COMPLETING THE CIRCLE

38 Stories of Mindful Connection

by Jon Berenson, Ph.D.

AuthorHouse™
1663 Liberty Drive
Bloomington, IN 47403
www.authorhouse.com
Phone: 1 (800) 839-8640

Published by AuthorHouse 05/03/2016

ISBN: 978-1-5246-0235-2 (sc)
ISBN: 978-1-5246-0236-9 (e)

Library of Congress Control Number: 2016905879

Print information available on the last page.

Any people depicted in stock imagery provided by Thinkstock are models,
and such images are being used for illustrative purposes only.
Certain stock imagery © Thinkstock.

This book is printed on acid-free paper.

Because of the dynamic nature of the Internet, any web addresses or links contained in this book may have changed since publication and may no longer be valid. The views expressed in this work are solely those of the author and do not necessarily reflect the views of the publisher, and the publisher hereby disclaims any responsibility for them.

authorHOUSE®

Dedication

To my soul friends: Linda, Donna, Peter, Don and Amy.

To each person with whom I have worked whose courage has inspired me to be a better human being.

To the Littles and the Bigs.

To Ruthi, from whom all good things have come.

Introduction

I think that most of us love stories. We read them nightly to our Little Ones; we go to movies; we read books; we watch a favorite serial drama; we listen to the adventure, challenge and emotion that our loved ones go through in the arc of their lives. In some ways, I believe, it is this draw to stories that "fit" for me as a profession, a career. As a psychologist and therapist, I listen to people's stories.

But I have come to know that it's not just any story that holds, inspires or moves me. The stories that do that for me are the ones that have to do with themes like family, love, heart, weakness, courage, redemption. In other words, stories about that crazy, spinning, opening and closing, fragile, tender and beautiful thing we call Real Life.

Every story in this book is true and was the result of my work with patients in my office for 45 years, or with participants at an Opening the Heart workshop which I have led for 36 years. I have changed the names, ages and circumstances of all the people involved in these stories in an attempt to protect their confidentiality. The Heart workshop originally started in 1976 at a place called Spring Hill in Ashby, Massachusetts by Dr. Robert Gass. When Spring Hill closed its' doors in 1998, the workshop continued, primarily at Omega Institute in Rhinebeck, New York and at Kripalu Institute for Yoga and Health in Stockbridge, Massachusetts.

The stories run the gamut of the real life continuum from tragedy and heartbreak to resilience and humor. But each story was chosen because it re-lit a flame inside me that yearns to become a more loving being on this tiny, crowded, hurting planet. So, hopefully, that speaks to the "stories" part of the book title.

What about the "mindful connection" part? Mindfulness has come to play a clear and increasingly important part of who I am and what I do for as long as I can remember. Mindfulness is the ability to stay with the breath in the present moment. This ability, I know, is critically important in being able to make conscious, loving choices rather than reactive ones. The reactive choices inevitably lead to more suffering. When we can make these more mindful choices, we have a better chance of staying in loving connection with others. And that, I believe, is what this whole "purpose of life" thing is really all about.

My hope is that in reading the stories, you may not just be moved, but, perhaps, open to a new possibility of becoming a more loving soul before your last breath goes out.

Jon

Table of Content

With a Trembling Heart

It is the yearning for wholeness that enables transformation to happen.

Very soon I'll be going back to Kripalu to help lead an Opening the Heart Workshop again. This workshop is the last weekend before the winter solstice (December 14-16). I think of this time in November and December as "The Dark Run"- a time of decreased natural light, a time of turning inward, of watching, waiting and contemplation- a time to prepare for the increased light to come back to us.

I have often referred to the contrast in the "energy" of a Friday night at Kripalu compared to Sunday morning. Friday night, as I look around at our first circle of the workshop, I often see doubt, fear, excitement, apprehension as I look into people's faces. By Sunday morning, the transformation is very dramatic. The energy in the room is lighter, peaceful, less heavy, and in people's faces I see no hiding, only compassion and kindness.

I find myself asking what exactly is it than enables this striking transformation to happen in about forty hours with a group of strangers. It is true that there is a warm and welcoming atmosphere at Kripalu. It is true that the leaders of the workshop are experienced and the safety and love they help to create is sincere and real. It is true that the music helps gather us in together. But this still doesn't answer, for me, what it is that helps bring about such dramatic change so quickly.

There is a prayer that I love that goes something like this:

> With all my heart have I gone out to seek You,
> And in going out, found You coming toward me.

I think the deeper answer about what causes such deep change at a workshop lies in this prayer: that it is not the singing or the welcoming or the building that, in themselves, transforms. Not really. I believe it is the yearning for wholeness that each participant brings, hesitantly, cautiously, with trembling heart, into the workshop on Friday. What we have, I think, at every workshop is a kind of biased sample. These are the brothers and sisters who have come because they yearn- they want serenity, they long to see kindness in a stranger's eyes. It is in the risk of "going out," of longing, of yearning that one hears the "echo," the answer that we are not alone. The key to the dramatic change is that when we enter that workshop space, we have all suffered and we yearn to be known, seen and embraced with our past suffering: we are willing to take a chance to connect with our deeper self.

It is the suffering that leads to the yearning, which leads to the risk to do something out of the ordinary - like coming to an experiential workshop in the Berkshire hills of Massachusetts with a roomful of people we've never seen before. It is easy, I think, to confuse the change agent and to give credit to "the workshop" or to the leaders or to "the place," but I think, truly, the real agent of change is carried into the workshop by each brave, trembling heart that dares to step into the extraordinary.

Just as the time of increased light at the start of the winter solstice would not be so yearned for without the Dark Run, so the opening of the heart would not be so powerful without the dark night of the soul that precedes it. In this time of increased light in the world, we wish you peacefulness of heart and we wish for each of us to come to the knowledge of our true selves. We are not alone- ever.

Come Alive

Becoming more loving to one another is the only answer
I know to the violence and suffering in the world.

On Friday afternoon, December 14th about 3:30, I was at Kripalu setting up the circle for the Opening the Heart Workshop which would start about 7:30 that night. I was in the Mountain View Room, facing west, and the sun was streaming in the windows. I like going to Kripalu early on a workshop weekend, to hang out, have an iced drink, set up the circle, check the lighting, read, sit quietly. My mind was calm and focused on the participants who would be sitting on those backjacks in a few short hours.

Just after 3:30, my friend, Peter, who was on his way to help lead the workshop, called to tell me the heartbreaking news he'd heard on the radio about the murders in New Town, Connecticut. As my mind began to wrap itself around this unbearable news, I had a vague awareness that I'd stopped breathing. Then came the thoughts: "Oh God, not again!... When, when will we have enough spine to stand up to gun lobbies and congressmen who are bought?... How many more dollars need to be cut for providing seriously mentally ill people, before we realize how much damage we are doing?..."

The thoughts came like an avalanche, released by the sudden shot of a loud gun. I watched my body continue to set up backjacks and pillows until a perfect circle was formed. Then I sat on one of the backjacks, breathed and let the circle begin to fill with the presence of 28 lives cut short in New Town. My heart began to beat as the circle continued to fill with twelve more souls killed in Aurora, Colorado; thirteen in Columbine; six at a Sikh temple in Oak Creek, Wisconsin; nine more souls entered the circle, killed in Manchester, Connecticut; seven more in Minneapolis this past year. The circle continued to fill, all the way back to our violent birth as a nation. I just sat, one beating heart, and I cried. No more thoughts, the mind finally still, the heart broken and aching. I cried til the crying stopped...

I'm not big on t-shirts or messages on t-shirts. I will go out of my way during the rare times I dare to shop for clothes by myself, to buy clothes that have no visible label or message. I know, I know- it's basically the same kind of snobbery that leads people to buy labels and messages. Anyway, when I was at Omega a few years ago, I saw a t-shirt with a message that I liked enough to buy: "Don't ask what the world needs. Ask what makes you come alive and do that. Because what the world needs are people who have come alive."

These words made me think of what Thich Nhat Hanh teaches: The foundations of one's being form the basis of one's actions. I believe what this great Zen master is talking about is his concept of "engaged Buddhism": before one can change the world for the good, one must open one's heart, still the mind and be in the present moment. This sometimes means bearing heartbreaking witness to deep suffering, as he did during the Vietnam War.

When I stopped the avalanche of thoughts and breathed and just attempted to sit with the broken heart, what became clearer to me in the moment was that I needed to do what I had come to Kripalu to do that weekend: to help people look into each other's eyes and see no difference- to be more compassionate and loving. So, I slowly got up from my cushion in the circle and saved the only thing I could save in that moment. I put tissue boxes around the circle, adjusted lighting, offered a prayer, blessed the souls in the center of the circle, bowed and waited quietly to welcome the first participants for the workshop.

Regrets

The best way to avoid regret is to do it now.

I read a list of things that people most regretted in their lives: not having traveled more, not having taken more risks, worrying too much about money and not enough about relationships. So, of course, I started doing my own R and R (review and regret). I wish I had tried more new things out of my comfort zone. I wish I had known how to forgive sooner. I wish I had been gentler on myself. I wish I had been less judgmental of others' failings. I wish I had enjoyed more sunrises. I wish I had worked harder at finding things to be grateful for every day.

It's a Monday morning, 7am and I am sitting with a friend. I should say, more specifically, that I am sitting for a friend and for his family. David died very unexpectedly last Friday. In my tradition, friends and loved ones sit with the body until burial so that the person who has died is never alone. I remember on Friday reading the e-mail: "We regret to inform you of the death of Dr. David M., father of Alan, Carolyn and Rachel; husband of Suzanne…" I had to read it several times to make sure it said what I feared it did. David was my age, which, of course, starts a whole other exercise for the busy mind.

He was a member of my men's book club and I liked him a lot. I like the men in our book club, but I always thought: "David is the best of us." He always recommended the best books. He was the one who seemed to have discovered these reading treasures before the rest of us and so when he recommended a book, it was because he'd read it and loved it. He introduced us to the author Erik Larsen and his best book *Devil in the White City*. David knew about Stieg Larsson and his famous trilogy (*Girl With the Dragon Tattoo*) before most of us had heard of the books.

David was very thoughtful about what he wanted us to read and didn't want us to read. When the group decided on a book of fiction about the Holocaust, David quietly refused to read it, saying that the Holocaust was awful enough as non-fiction and he didn't need to put himself through made-up horror of the event. He didn't judge anyone else who chose differently.

I considered David a friend even though we didn't hang out or spend a lot of time together. I remember years ago he called me and asked to speak to me about something personal. I was surprised and more than happy to sit with him one night while he opened his heart about a heartbreaking rift with his daughter. I felt good that I could listen and offer things for him to think about.

I always felt that my wife and I should invite David and Suzanne for dinner because I knew it would be a good foursome. But I just never did. I also felt that there was more to David than he ended up showing you- that there was more of a story than you ever really knew about. And it turned out to be true. I never knew that he'd had a stroke about a year ago and I never knew he'd had a heart condition and was on blood thinners. He never spoke of it.

The things I knew about him, I liked. He was sensitive, smart, funny, loved by his wife and children, loved by his patients and respected by friends and community. He was a great dad, a good physician and I regret not being a better friend- not taking the time to know him more deeply.

But when I get up shortly from sitting for my friend, I will honor him by going out into the cold, gray morning, with no regrets, and being grateful beyond words for the beauty of it all.

My Religion

Why wait to practice kindness?

Friday March 15th was the first day that friends and family began to have an awareness that Sunil Trapathi was "missing." Sunil is an Indian-American student at Brown University in Providence. His parents live in Pennsylvania but they had been in Rhode Island to help in the heartbreaking search for their son. Sunil has an older brother and sister who have been working tirelessly in and around Providence hanging pictures on store fronts, on telephone poles and in meeting places. They describe him as a wonderful brother who had been on a medical leave of absence from Brown because he was struggling with depression. The day before he was listed as missing, he spoke to his grandmother and aunt, who both love him. Over the past six weeks, a whole community came to love him. On Facebook, people, many who'd never met Sunil, sent messages of love written on a left hand or a right hand: "Sunil, do not give up hope"; "You are not alone"; "I, too, have suffered in the past"; "Don't give up, you are loved." The fact that a whole community could come together, to help search and to help send love and relieve suffering made an impression on me.

One night, as my wife and I left a restaurant on Thayer Street near Brown, we saw Sunil's smiling face on a telephone pole and we felt an ache in our hearts for his family. Many in the community came to meet Sunil's family when they knocked on doors to ask if their son, Sunil, had been seen. All leads came to nothing until a Brown student, a rower, found Sunil's body in the Seekonk River. Yes, there was some closure, but the circle of friends and kind caring souls turned their attention from searching to comforting. There was so much compassionate caring and love. People who were strangers now had a common bond and would smile and talk to one another....

The news reports said it was "like no other week in the history of Boston." Lockdowns, late night shootouts, grenades and police chases. Murder, senseless deaths and horrible injuries of people wanting to simply enjoy a beautiful spring day and an annual tradition of the Boston Marathon. The word that witnesses kept repeating was "surreal" which means "having an oddly dreamlike quality." They were referring not just to the death, horror and maiming, but to acts of incredible heroism and kindness: people running *toward* the explosions to get the wounded medical help or simply to apply a tourniquet. Only minutes before the explosions, these people were strangers, who may well not have smiled at each other in passing or said hello, were now connected in a life and death drama.

So I wondered why many of us wait for an excuse or a disaster in order to be kind. Why not practice it in some small way right now: letting a driver go ahead of us instead of getting home fourteen seconds early; an offer in the parking lot to help an older shopper load their car with bags; a smile as we walk past someone on the street. Why wait? Do you remember how connected and friendly so many of us felt after 9/11? The Dalai Lama once said, when asked what his religion was: kindness. Maybe we could practice that religion when it's not a life or death matter, because, in truth, in many ways, it is a matter of life and death.

Creating Godness

Redemption happens when we open a dark place to the light.

Though I've only seen Sam and Jenny together in my office for a short while, I had seen Sam alone for almost three years. He had been married before, and Sam's life had not been an easy one. It may have been blessed, probably was, but it was one of those lives where you need to wait a whole long time before you say "Wow! it was hard to see those ragged early years as anything but suffering, but now I see how it all fits together."

Perhaps the most painful chapter of Sam's story was that he lost a child- his only daughter (two other sons). I really liked Sam a lot and my heart ached for all the ways his life seemed to be unfair- too jagged. Then he met Jenny: "She's kind, Jon, and she makes me laugh. She's pretty and she really loves me. Me! Can you believe it?" They loved each other very much but Sam began to see some things he hadn't seen during the months their closeness and love grew.

The main issue seemed to be around his 'leaving'. It might be for bowling night or a business meeting, but he noticed she would become unreasonably irritable. Even she would admit, with some time to gain perspective, that her behavior was reactive and even blaming of Sam. I asked her to tell me about her dad. She told me her parents divorced when she was about eleven and it was one of those ugly, blood-on-the-walls divorce that took hostages of anyone on the battlefield. Jenny said "My mother turned me against my father." I asked her to tell me more because I sensed there was more. Her eyes began to fill as she told me that she could still remember as "clear as if it was yesterday," when she screamed at her dad that she never wanted to see him again and she recalled the broken look on his face as she slammed her bedroom door in his face, and refused to open it. Out of loyalty to her mom, Jenny did not speak to her father again, as he died of a sudden massive heart attack less than three years later.

By now she was sobbing and trying to talk to him through the almost thirty years that had passed. "I'm so sorry Daddy...." I asked her to close her eyes and I asked Sam to sit directly in front of her. With Jenny's eyes closed, I asked her to remember her dad's younger face, and to bring it into sharp focus as she remembered him that last day. Tears fell down her face. I asked her to see her father's face when she opened her eyes.... And she did. "Daddy I miss you. I'm so sorry..." Jenny emptied her heart and when she was done, I asked her to breathe and listen to her dad's voice coming through Sam. I knew that Sam had lost a daughter, but Jenny didn't know the details because Sam had only ever talked

about them in my office. His daughter was sixteen and overdosed on drugs and he never had a chance to say good-bye to his "little girl"- until now. He looked at Jenny and saw his daughter's face and he said "I was always with you. I never left. And I will always be with you. I miss you, too, and I will always love you so very much. What I need you to hear now is that I will never leave you and that there is nothing to forgive." By now, the tears were falling from Sam's eyes, too, as well as mine and I thought "If we don't stop this soon, we're gonna be ankle-deep from all the tears." But they were good tears, healing waters....

So why am I telling you this story? I wrote a piece called "Praying with Beginner's Eyes" and I realized that, for me, praying in that way is one path for creating Godness. That day, in my office, Sam and Jenny's courage in making a descent and in opening a dark place to light- that, too, created Godness right in my office, before my grateful eyes.

Installing My GPS

You can always find your way somewhere by going home first.

"The initial mystery of every journey is how the traveler got to the starting point to begin with." ~ Louise Bogan

Have you ever been really lost? No, I don't mean in an existential way where your soul yearns for a way home. I mean when you've taken the wrong turn on the Mass Pike and you end up in Worcester instead of Boston and it's 45 minutes before you even think that if you were going to Boston (east), then the sun would not be behind you at 4 pm, instead of directly in your eyes.

My son and I have a dominant FAI gene ("Fuggetaboutit!") when it comes to finding our way someplace. We have actually come to use our own Berenson Positioning System which calls for us to go home first and then find our way from there. This actually works pretty well, except that we are often hours (or days) late getting somewhere.

You might say "My God, Jon, why aren't you using GPS? They're really inexpensive now?" And I would say, in my technophobe-rehearsed way "I don't think so. I'd have to go back to graduate school for two semesters to learn how to use it." Then you might say something that no one should ever say to a technophobe: "No, Jon, it's really simple." Because saying this to me only makes me feel like a heavy brick when I just can't figure out how to use it.

So I start thinking about GPS in a different way. I am really good at languages and I have a very good ear for words, sounds and accents. I was driving on the New Jersey Turnpike once and I stopped to ask the toll taker where the Elizabeth exit was. After he told me, I asked him if he was from Bristol, England, where I'd once spent a summer. His face brightened and he said "How did you know?"

I do believe this whole technology deal is nothing more than a language that I'm having a hard time learning. I started thinking about the basic principles of GPS and translated them to my own "language" and personal context. What I do when I feel disconnected from self, others and the world is that I start by going home. For me that's reconnecting with breath and going inside and finding a way to calm myself, waiting for solid ground and perspective to come back.

Then I ask myself where it is that I want to go. I want to be reunited with my source. I want to feel lighter, more positive, grateful. This is what I call my *intention*. On the GPS, it's the address I want to end up at. Well, I have learned some skills along this highway. I practice being the witness of my experience, my *lostness*. I become aware of how disconnected I feel and I practice saying "Isn't this interesting." By practicing watching my experience, I step out of the parade and, even for a few moments, observe the parade from the stands. I keep attention on my breath. I may invite an experience of gratitude. I may practice some positive self talk. The scenery doesn't always change. This isn't a "trick" to feel better. The key to staying on the right roads is to keep practicing being in the present.

I have come to call this my own GPS (God Positioning System), finding my way to a destination by using intention, skillful means, the breath, and continuing to bring myself back to the present. I think, actually, that going home first to find my way somewhere may not be such a bad idea.

Bowing to Kiss the Ground

What holy things do we not see every day?

So, as I understand it, Moses was at the top of the mountain for a long time. Can you imagine hanging with the Major Dude for that long? He must have had every bad karma and inclination to badness just burned out of him, wouldn't you think? Anyway, I guess the shepherd was up there too long for the flock and the crowds below started to lose the vision. Doubt crept in on little camel feet. They started partying and pretty soon they naturally went to the ancient bad habit of golden calf building. Well, when Moses finally came down and saw the goings on, he was, excuse the term,, "pissed as a New York cabdriver," and he smashed the tablets to the ground right then and there and he turned around and started his march back up to the top. So, what's my point?... I always wondered about those first broken tablets. What was written on them? Was it the same ten commandments? What happened to those broken holy pieces with God's word written on them?

The scene I imagine is George and Marge on vacation taking a hike up Mount Sinai and George looks down and calls out to Marge: "Hey Marge! Have a look at this. It looks like very old pieces of stone with maybe some writing on them." "George, all these rocks are the same. Come and see this beautiful view from here." And George's attention passes to a natural scene of wonder.

And it makes me think, what other holy things do we pass over every day? In some Eastern traditions, it's called seeing with "Beginner's Eyes"- seeing things as if for the first time. When we bring careful attention to anything, there can be a blessing. It really is a practice of gratitude and I believe it can start anywhere you are. Don't move, don't go to a beautiful place, just close your eyes, go inside and breathe. The breath is a holy thing. Nothing in life happens without the breath. Watch as it comes in and fills the lungs and become aware of exactly when the inbreath changes to the outbreath, all the way to the end, and, again, becomes the inbreath.

Now try using your eyes to settle on whatever is around you, something you may have seen a thousand times before. This time see it for the first time. See every detail of it so that if you closed your eyes, you could describe it to every perfect detail. Change your attention to the sense of smell. Maybe you need to approach something that has an aroma. A flower in your garden will do. Smell it as if for the first time. Let all of your awareness take it in.

Go for a short walk and feel the miracle of legs moving your body. An appreciation of the mundane by bringing full attention to it is a kind of prayer of gratitude. Don't miss a thing. Take it all in. Leave nothing out. Pay attention. Meister Eckhart, a 14th century German mystic, said that "Coincidences happen more when I pray." When we pay attention- really pay attention- in the moment, we are, as the poet, Rumi, says "bowing down to kiss the ground."

So what are the takeaways here? Keep the faith Sweet One- don't go building golden calves; look for the holy in the Everyday and make it a sacred practice; pay attention as well as you can to every moment you are given the gift of breath.

Letter From the Front

I never really was meant to fit into the 21st century.

So I thought I would just share, briefly, how the war is going. That would be the war to have me enter the 21st century with some dignity. The short answer is: could be better. When I first bought a Mac and had my first year of 1:1 classes, I'm guessing I was closer to 1987 than the late 60's where I started, and I renewed my lessons for another year. Here's the thing, though: I never got it before that the 21st century is also moving ahead and, unfortunately, faster than me. Here's what I mean.

I have an old Verizon flip phone. So I had this panic that if I ever wash my phone in the washing machine or even just lose it, I was not going to be able to replace it because they're not made anymore!... "What you need young man is this phone with 64 giggle bites of expandable memory and an eight megapixel remote camera and a touch screen GPS." As my eyes glazed over, I decided it would just be easier to keep my phone away from the washing machine.

Here's a second example of how I think, even while I'm moving ahead, I'm getting behind. One night at home I decided to watch the movie "Babel" with Brad Pitt. It tells four distinctly different stories in four different countries and then begins to weave the stories together into a coherent tale. Because the settings were in Morocco, Tokyo, Mexico and the U.S., three quarters of the dialogue was unintelligible to me. There were no subtitles and so I was very confused in trying to follow any kind of story line.

Then I realized that the language mix-up was exactly the point: that one could still make sense of the plot even when the languages were so confusing. The point of the biblical story of Babel was that God confounded the language because of man's pride.

So I settled in to make sense of what was happening even without being able to follow one language through the plot. Until... my son came into the room, looked at the movie, looked at me and said "Dad, what are you doing?" I explained to him my perceptive insight. He shrugged and, as he left the room, he said "If you decide you want subtitles, all you do is press 'menu' and click 'option A'..."

Maybe I was just meant to stay in the late 60's all along.

Praying With Beginner's Eyes

The ache and yearning for connection is, itself, a deep prayer.

I read something that amazed me recently and I'd like to share it with you. Michael Merzenich is a neuroscientist who developed Posit Science which is a San Francisco company, one of the first companies ten years ago to enter the new field of brain fitness. Here's what he said: "When you're young and you see something surprising, your eyes are attracted to it. You're bright-eyed, literally." For older people in their 60's and 70's, their peripheral vision is three-quarters as panoramic as that of a twenty year old. Here's what amazed me: he said "We want to train your eyes to be more childlike.... We can take a person of any age and restore their sparkiness."

The light that went on immediately in my head is the thought that what he's really talking about is learning to look at things with "beginner's eyes." This is the phrase that meditators, behavioral researchers, psychologists use in re: to helping people develop mindfulness practices. Just take a moment wherever you are and look at something inside or outside a room. Really, just look at it and breathe and then, keep looking at it and breathing. Just "be with" it. You don't need to redesign it or think of a better place to put it, just contemplate it. Be, in the present moment, with it and see it as if for the very first time, letting everything you "know" about it drop away: its function, its history, its meaning in your life. Just let it be and let yourself be, with it....

If you've started to read this new paragraph, stop. Go back to the object you've been contemplating and stay with it for ten minutes (approximate the time, don't keep checking your watch!)....

Okay, so the main point I want to make is about prayer. For many years I have had a daily prayer life: before each meal, when I enter my therapy office and when I leave it, when I feel grateful, when I see a wonder or a miracle for the first time, when I am graced with serenity.

My dear friend, Peter, gave me a book for my birthday called *Help. Thanks. Wow* by Anne Lamott: the three essential prayers. What I loved about the book was her challenge to make prayer real, authentic. So I began to look at my own prayer practice. I took inventory: Gratitude, yup, check; lift our suffering, check; watch over and protect loved ones, got it. I began to see that my prayer life had aged. It was not authentic or real, it had become a rote practice, a covering the bases.

I knew I needed to get back to being real, in the moment, to feeling the yearning for connection with whatever you may want to call a higher power or God. My belief is that real prayer, with heart, the juicy prayer, is the authentic ache and yearning for connection. For me, it's not a conversation with God. It's the yearning or the "call" that actually is the response, or echo, of our prayer.

So I began my new prayer practice with a question: How am I feeling inside? Really, how am I feeling? Rather than check off the usual boxes, I was determined to be more honest with whatever was true for me in that moment: raw anger, outrage, grief, elation, relief, peacefulness- to really bring it gently into my embrace and awareness and just be with it, give voice to it, as much as possible, without self conscious judgment. In other words, to see it with new, honest, beginner's eyes, lover's eyes. This practice has made me, I believe, more real, more whole, more able to see with a wider panorama the beautiful, translucent whole of the life I've been given.

Getting Some Things Right for Halloween

Taking off our mask is a courageous thing we can only do in a very safe place.

"It's never too late to have a happy childhood."   ~Ken Kesey

In my therapy practice, I see a 64 year old man who is dying of liver cancer. John tells me that he asked his oncology doctors at Dana Farber in Boston to be "straight" with him in re: to longevity. John said "They told me I have three to maybe twenty months to live." He added "That was ten months ago." He is a very successful businessman, impeccably dressed in clothes that fit him perfectly. He tells me this stoically, without a tear or any drama. And yet, there is a tenderness to his voice when he adds that he wants to "get some things right" before he dies. He explains that he would like to get closer to his two children and also to their partners. "My whole life, I never knew how to make time for John."

What this meant was that he grew up in a home without a lot of emotion or warmth. But he learned to work and be productive from the time he was fourteen. And he was successful at harvesting recognition from his accomplishments. "I had no idea that maybe I should aim for a little more balance in my life" - to try to grow love for both self and others. His disclosure that he never made time for himself was poignant to me. He'd never just vegged out in front of the tv with his feet up, munching popcorn or went to the movies, or took a stroll in the park with his son on a beautiful early spring day- never took time to just enjoy himself.

Two weeks ago John asked his daughter-in-law, Suzanne, to go with him to meet with the social worker at Dana Farber for some "planning" to bring closure to some of the details of his life. Frank, the social worker, suggested that John may want to write instructions for his family regarding who John wanted to be pall bearers at the funeral, and also for John to make a list of who should be notified of his passing. As John gave the names, Suzanne wrote them down. And as John continued, his eyes filled up, and he became quiet as the names of loved ones caught in his throat and more tears came.

Suzanne looked up, her eyes also filled with tears. She'd never seen John cry before. At lunch after the meeting, John thanked Suzanne for being there, telling her how much it meant to him to have her there. She hugged him hard and long and said how much his tears meant to her and they cried, again, together...

Someone told me that in this country, we spend $300 million dollars a year on costumes for pets for Halloween. And I thought of how much we spend on ourselves, too, to put on costumes and masks for this one day each year. But really, when Halloween is over, we take the masks off, but make sure that the other masks we wear year round are still well in place. I thought "Where in our lives do we feel safe enough, courageous enough, to take off those well-fitted masks and risk showing who we really are, how we really feel."

It occurred to me that at that meeting with the social worker, John really was, finally, taking time for himself to be real with his daughter-in-law, and what a gift it was to them both. But, even more, what it might mean to John's son and grandchildren to be able to see behind the curtain. Since that meeting, John has committed to getting other "things" in order. He is meeting his son for breakfast once a week and he has invited his daughter to go with him to a conference on "Living Beyond Cancer." I have such admiration for John and his courage to not give up learning how to love even at the end of his life.

Reunion and Separation

We really do need reminders that life is short.

When I went to my 50th high school reunion, I had many mixed feelings: would I recognize people, would they recognize me? How well had I aged compared to everyone else? Would I still have a crush on Arlene Mattarazzo? Would Francene still have a crush on me, or even remember that she'd had one? Who remembered what, how would we look, was it a mistake to come? Then I remembered to breathe and came back to the moment and marveled at how quickly we could still descend into the busy, negative mind. Then, I made a decision to just have a fun time.

In my therapy practice, when I teach mindfulness strategies, I will often speak about learning to develop perspective- to watch the parade rather than march in it. In regards to my reunion, "marching in the parade" meant getting lost in the worry, doubt, comparing, fretting. When we do march in the parade there is a lot of drama, and when there's drama, there's always suffering close by. When we are able to watch the parade from the grandstand, there's less drama, and, therefore, less suffering. So I decided to just see each person who came before me that night as an interesting form of the Beloved, of God- and that I could just have a good time with the dance.

There was Richard who was one of the first to marry in our high school class, and he married my wife's best friend, Louise. They married young and divorced before I even got married, and Louise, a high school beauty, was now a depressed, aging alcoholic. There was my friend, Ted, kind, heart of gold, a little awkward, and never married. There was Linda who screamed when she saw me and hugged me and said "Oh Jon, you haven't changed a bit!" And I walked away saying to myself "I've never in my life, ever, seen that woman before!" And there was my life long friend Jay, with his wife of forty years, now a grandparent three times. How did that happen to us who played stickball in my backyard after school and went to summer camp together?

And then, I found myself standing in front of the Memorium Board. Here were all the people in my class who were no longer living: Carl, who died right after graduation; Tom, who was walking on the ice on Bullough's Pond when he fell through and drowned.... And there was my closest friend, Billy. Bill's family was my second family. If I was not home, I would likely be at his house, hanging with the guys. We were there one Saturday afternoon just being fourteen year old bad boys when our friend, Lester, called, and we passed the phone around giving him a hard time. Just seconds after the call

ended, the phone rang again and I said "Give me that phone.... What do you want you little shithead!?"... "I'd like to speak to my son, Jon..." "Yes, Mrs. Myers."

It took me many weeks before I had the courage to show my face at Billy's house. Mr. Myers answered my hesitant knock and he said to me "Billy's in the den.... And the little shithead is in the kitchen if you want to say hi."

Billy and I were always together- always getting into mischief. Well, not entirely true. "We" would get into mischief, but he was the one who always got caught. In that long moment standing before his picture, I had such a deep ache of missing him. When I thought of his death all those years ago, and looked around me at 50 years passing in the blink of an eye, I thought "Do we really need reminders that life is short?" The answer, I think, is that we do. We keep needing reminders to wake up, to come alive, to watch the parade and to try to stay in the moment. And in this moment, I was sad and grateful and aware of the separation from a friend of the heart.

Union and Reunion

Looking deep takes patience and courage.

A while ago I went to my 50th high school reunion. It was a great night, seeing old friends, meeting people who weren't friends but maybe, after connecting with them that night, realized they could have been. It was a hoot hearing how others had remembered or experienced me back in high school. Charlotte gave me a huge hug and pulled me over to meet her husband, James, whom I had played baseball with in junior high school (now known as middle school). I had a crush on Charlotte for three weeks my junior year of high school.

So, in high school and college I lived for baseball. I remember looking out the window of my English class on the first floor to see how quickly the snow was melting because the sooner the field was dry, the sooner we would be out there breathing spring and throwing a ball and running the bases. My senior year David tried out for third base, my position. He was dating the coach's daughter, Susie. The coach, "Fergy," was a tough, old-school guy who took baseball very seriously. If he saw you throwing a snowball before practice started on March 1st, he'd keep you out of practice for two weeks for risking throwing your arm out.

Well, the end of March I was cut from the team and I never really got over it. I didn't know what to do with myself after school. I was stunned. I didn't feel I deserved to be cut and I blamed David.... Cut to the reunion and I was talking with some of the guys who had played sports, remembering old times, telling stories, laughing, enjoying reliving memories. Then David came over. "Hi Jon." "Hi David." We all continued to talk but I was a little distracted and I began to think: "Jon, you're 68. The only way to be at peace with this is to go for it."

So I said, "David, can I ask you a question?" "Sure, Jon." "David, did you really think you were better than me at third base our senior year?" He looked at me, puzzled. "What do you mean Jon?" "David, Fergy cut me from the team senior year. You ended up playing third base." "Jon, I didn't play third base. I sat on the bench most of the year. Terry played third."

I was really stunned. It took me a minute to take in this new information. "Really? You didn't start at third?" "No, I only got into a couple of games." "David, I'm sorry, but I'm really happy." And I couldn't help being struck by living my life for fifty years with a myth: not ever having gotten over something that never happened. I got up and I scanned the room looking at faces and remembering. How many other myths for how many others in the room? There was Steve, always on the fringe in high school, never part of the crowd I was friendly with- never someone I took too seriously, or took the time to get to know. Steve, who came back from three tours in Vietnam, a shattered man, in trouble with alcohol and alienated from his wife and kids.

I thought "wouldn't it have been something to look beneath the masks we held carefully in place fifty years ago- to be able to see deeper." Yes, probably would have been some trip! But more importantly,, in this moment, asking myself if I'm any more skilled at looking deeper than the masks or wounds- deep enough to see the compassion and humanity we all share.

Walking Away From a Miracle

Can we actually create miracles if we practice kindness?

One cannot stay on the summit forever.
So why bother in the first place? Just this:
What is above knows what is below-
But what is below does not know what is above.
One climbs and one sees-
One descends and sees no longer.
When one can no longer see
One can at least still remember.   ~ *Mount Analogue* Rene Daumal

There is a beautiful piece of music written by Hector Berlioz called *L'Enfance du Christ*. Within it is a piece called the Departure of the Shepherds. In that poignant scene the shepherds are leaving the scene of Jesus' birth. So in this winter solstice season of reflection and turning inward, of the Dark Run, I wondered what it must have been like to walk away from a miracle. Had I ever really experienced a miracle myself? As I ask this question, writing at my grandfather's roll top desk, I look up six inches at pictures of my son, my daughter, my wife, and I just smile. So what really is a miracle? It is, I think, a divine descension of grace, undeserved, but, nonetheless, bestowed. Meister Eckhart, a fourteenth century theologian, said "Miracles seem to happen more when I pray."

So maybe a miracle is a coincidence, seen through a spiritual perspective. Then is a miracle something unusual and amazing that happens and we witness or experience it, or does it happen more from inside out? If we are awake, conscious, looking for the good, or miracles, we, in a true sense; create them. This view is in alignment with what the new mindfulness researchers in the field of happiness tell us.

Let's go back to the shepherds: how could they possibly return to their ordinary lives? How could their lives not be transformed? They would see everything differently through eyes of having seen a world-changing transformation.

At the end of an Opening the Heart workshop, we read to participants Rene Duamal's poem (above). It's a way of reminding us that the ascension of the mountain is, in and of itself, of value even when we must, inevitably, descend again from the summit. It's of value because by having taken the miracle in, we have become changed. We have changed even though the natural rhythms continue of life's openings and closings. To each living thing there is a season, an opening and a closing: the breath, the seasons, the day, the natural Life-Death-Life cycle. On December 9th I looked out my office window at my serenity garden and I saw a miracle. There it was in the eight inch turquoise pot sitting on my garden wall: one yellow pansy. On December 10th it was gone, but I *had* seen and I will remember that bright flower until I plant again in April.

Flying and Other Small Miracles

One day I would really love to flap my arms, lift off the ground and glide all day on warm air currents.

I read about a survey where people were asked if they could choose a 'super power', what would it be. By far, the two most popular answers were 1) to be invisible and 2) to be able to fly. I didn't have to think twice about this one. For me, it would be flying. In terms of being invisible, just too much legal, bureaucratic red tape. For example, if you're invisible, do there have to be stipulations that the clothes you're wearing are included in the deal, because I just would not want to have gone through the airline checkpoints without detection and then find myself on a twelve hour fight to Hawaii sitting naked, with a priest to my left and an 81 year old grandmother going to a Tupperware convention on my right, just because I didn't know how long the invisibility lasted!

Or what's the deal if I'm holding someone's hand? Do they get to be invisible too? Because I would not want to find out after the fact that my wife is slow dancing alone at a family wedding. You know what I'm saying? No, for me, flying is, hands down, so to speak, the way to go.

Some of my all-time favorite moments are spent on my deck in Westport watching the ospreys soar over the river looking for a meal. Or, on that same deck, watching the hummingbird drink from the feeder six feet from my chair. It is nothing but magical, watching her dart and flit from feeder to cypress tree and back. And I know she's coming because I can hear the whir of her wings. Did you know that there is only one species of hummingbird east of the Mississippi? It's the ruby-throated hummingbird.

When I go clamming in the river, I love to dig my toes into the mud to find cherrystones and little necks. I watch the wind patterns on the water and the sun reflecting off the river. But what is most enchanting is to watch the swans take off from the water, or to see the great blue herons and egrets soaring overhead. What an amazing feeling that must be to be able to fly!

And as I'm digging clams and thinking about it, I wonder "Is it an amazing feeling for the great blue or egret or the magical hummingbird?" I conclude, a little sadly, that it's probably *not* an amazing feeling for them. It's just who they are and it's what they do. I would be ecstatic, I reason, if I could be that fabulous bird and have an awareness of flying - of being able to do something so new and different and wondrous!

So, if it's bringing awareness and consciousness to something that makes it so special, seeing with beginner's eyes, then all I really have to do is bring my full attention to sitting here in my chair, in this moment, and breathe in the joy of my writing these words, watching the hummingbird and nuthatch and the kayaker on the river. I only have to bring my attention to digging my toes into the soft mud and feeling the warmth of the sun on my face and watching ospreys feed their chicks in their platform nests on the marsh in the river.

Jon Kabbat Zinn, the psychologist, once defined healing as the process of bringing one's attention to what is going on in the present moment... Still, I would, one day, so dearly love to flap my arms and lift off and see the world below and glide on warm air currents and be absolutely at one with the universe.... Actually, I realize I can already do that. Some traditions call it 'samadhi', some, the 'oceanic experience'. New researchers exploring altered states of consciousness call these states 'entheogenic'. I call them peak experiences and they can, all by themselves, make my life soar.

A Smile at the Checkout Counter

Be prepared to give what you want most to receive.

After the 9/11 tragedy, I remember that for many weeks afterward, walking on public streets was a whole new experience. What I remember is that many times people made eye contact with each other and even smiled and I asked myself what was it that caused this poignant, deeper connection with strangers that I had walked past hundreds of times before without any eye contact or recognition or kind greeting. I'm really convinced that 9/11 caused a deeper recognition of ourselves. I think what we recognized after 9/11, or after any hard life jolt, was our common humanity, our deep connectedness and our vulnerability.

I find myself coming back to the theme of perspective. I see a patient who is dying of inoperable pancreatic cancer. He came to see me one morning and the weather was rainy and cold. In an unconscious moment, perhaps to make small talk or to put him at ease, I said "Pretty dreary weather." He smiled and said "You know, Jon, I have a different way of thinking about the weather now. If it's cold, I put on an extra sweater. If it's wet, I take an umbrella.... I'm just glad to be alive." His words brought me into an immediate place of understanding and perspective in the same way, I think, that 9/11 brought such hard clarity to many of us....

I don't know how many of you may be lucky enough to be a grandparent, but I became a "Grumpy" for the second time. Don't worry, I am not going to bore you with the amazing cuteness and accomplishments of these Beings of Light (although watching my fifteen month old on Facetime take her first two steps alone, and hearing about my new granddaughter turning over at not even one month old- Get outta town!) No, I'm taking this in a different direction that, again, brings us back to perspective.

I was at the checkout counter at the grocery store where I shop and a young woman checking out was carrying an adorable 4 month old baby, while at the same time, trying to get out her credit card. The baby was facing back, looking at the next person in line, a middle-aged man. The man made a big, warm, kind smile at the baby, and I thought "What is there about a baby that evokes this automatic, kind welcoming?" In my mind I erased the baby and tried to imagine the man's same kind smile toward the mother (now without the baby). Doesn't work, does it? Who knows, but my guess is that the smile would have been ignored or misunderstood, not taken in. It did occur to me that every one of us still carries that baby, or small inner child within us that keeps looking at the world and asking "Do you like me?" And when we experience that kind smile, that unconditional welcome, we tend to feel seen, held, accepted, even loved.

There is, I think, a spiritual principle that says we must be prepared to give what we most want to receive. So, I decided to try being the Prime Mover. That is, I committed for one week to just give a friendly smile to anyone I saw that I didn't know. Rather than waiting to see if they would welcome me, I gave the welcome, the kindness first. What I did was I aimed the smile beneath the adult exterior, the mask, directly to that adorable baby inside. I really experienced feeling better by "being the change we want to be." Many times, my smile was returned just as that little baby smiled naturally at being welcomed at the checkout counter.

I Don't Ever Want to Leave This Place

"Are you looking for me? I'm in the next seat, the next breath." ~ Kabir

If you've never been to an Opening the Heart workshop before, I'd like to, very briefly, describe what it's like. Over the course of a weekend, a group, usually of strangers, come together to make what I call a "descent"- to face buried demons, hurts, wounds and to give them a proper, peaceful and honorable burial: to be done with them. No, I agree: why would anyone actually choose to do this? Doesn't a kayak trip or a Vermont B+B sound more appealing? I agree.

But I want to tell you that there is also something transformational and exhilarating about going to one's own edge, taking this kind of a risk to be seen without the mask or your best hair- to really allow yourself to look into another's eyes and see no difference in a setting that is constructed to be very safe and loving. So, usually, not always, on a Sunday, right after the workshop ends, there is a powerful feeling of openness, compassion and love.

Well, after the last workshop, as people were hugging and saying good bye, I happened to notice one participant, sitting against the wall crying quietly. I slowly came over, gave her some kleenex and just sat with her. I didn't say a word. When she could finally breathe and speak, she looked into my eyes and said "I don't ever want to leave this place." I breathed. More tears came. She tried a smile and asked "Do I have to leave?" I held her hands and waited a long while before saying "Yes." I looked into her eyes again and said "It's important that you go back and take with you what you found here." She just looked at me, held my hands tight and would not let go....

For over twenty years, from about 1976 to 1998, we did the workshop at our own special place called Spring Hill in Ashby, Massachusetts. It was an idyllic place in a beautiful, hand-built rustic barn overlooking a forest and hills. We often talked about the "magic" that we believed was held in the pine board walls, vaulted ceilings and warm, purple wall to wall rug. It really did feel like just being in that place was calming and serene, a kind of coming home, even before the workshop would begin. When Spring Hill closed, many of us on staff really did believe that the "magic" would be impossible to re-create anywhere else. We were wrong....

As I looked into "Carol's" eyes, I told her that I did not want her to confuse the "miracle" with the inner transformation she had experienced that weekend. I think that she had come to believe that the "miracle" occurred because of the beauty and peacefulness of Kripalu or Omega- the music of the workshop, the kindness of staff, the great and healthy food served, sometimes in blissful silence. I told her that the real miracle occurred because of the awesome power of taking a risk to be real and present with buried pain. The miracle was the inner transformation- the incredible perspective that comes when one is able to really see from the summit. Why would anyone actually choose to come to Kripalu or Omega, to step out of the ordinary and into something extraordinary like making a descent? And why, after rising from the descent to come to the summit, would one wish to ever leave that place?

The poet Kabir said "Are you looking for me? I'm in the next seat, in the next breath." Yes, I know, it's a bit of a cliche, but, nonetheless true: the miracle of the transformation was always inside us, not in the circumstances of the Opening the Heart workshop, or the songs, or the staff, or the food or the natural beauty. Always inside us. So I told Carol that I also wished for her to never have to leave "this place," but to be really brave in not waiting for the "place" to align with our expectations, but to actively take steps to get back in touch with the greatness that is always a breath away.

A Careful Weeder

For me, the skilled weeder holds a special place of honor.

One morning when I walked my dog, Fenway, I felt it in the air: the more moderate air temperature of forty degrees, the sun coming up over the tree line later in the morning, the cardinals and robins chirping and looping through the air. I know, I know, this sounds like the delusions of an over-hardened native New Englander mistaking a temporary mild weather front from a true change of seasons in early February. But I did feel it. And because I did, I started looking at the tired, overgrown gardens on my walk, imagining turning the ground over in two months, clearing out the old and dead, making room for the new life that would come.

I'm a weeder by nature. I was hard-wired and designed to sit in a part of a garden and hand pick weeds so the rightful inheritors could take their place. I can remember doing this since I was a boy, always feeling things aligning properly when a patch had been cleared. If you're a careful and serious weeder, this is not so easy as it may look. You need to know weeds and how they sometimes deceive by looking like new sprouts of flowers or plants. You have to know how to pick the weed out, going deep, getting the whole root so it doesn't grow back. And you should really know what to do with the weed so it will help in the compost to fertilize new oriental lilies, hibiscus, astilbe or rose bush.

I did my apprenticeship with my dad who, himself, was a master weeder. Whenever the family was running around packing things up for a family outing, I knew where my dad would be waiting for us. He would be sitting on the front lawn quietly removing every dandelion, one at a time, with his forked, yellow-handled tool, making a mound of the pulled weeds. When my dad died, I remember searching in the garage for the only thing I really wanted- the yellow-handled weed remover, and then finding a place for it on the shelf of my own garage.

Becoming a weeder was not just a way of finding a place of serenity and renewal for me. Yes, I love sitting in the sun in a garden and taking my time to make an area clean and healthy. Yes, I do really get a sense of accomplishment and satisfaction from seeing something look and grow healthy.

But I have been humbled and grateful to have learned that weeding had also become my profession. In my therapy practice, working with patients, I sit and try to help them clear their own weeds. I've come to accept that they need to identify which are the weeds and which the plants. They have to have the temperament, or courage, to want to remove

them and they have to know how to go deep enough to remove the root. They have to be able to use discernment to tell the difference between a weed and a growing sprout that may, if they're patient, grow into something beautiful and unique. They have to, in a real sense, become careful and skilled gardeners themselves. I think when I am helpful, it's because I can support them to know when it's time to pull and when it's time to wait. Years ago, I had been working with a woman for four years who had been continuously traumatized by sexual abuse when she was a little girl. One day in therapy, she said to me, "It's time, Jon…. It's time to confront the man who did this." I said, "Please don't." She asked why. I told her not to confront him unless she was prepared to have him deny that it had ever happened. She cried, nodded and waited for six months until she was ready.

I sometimes think that in our culture the weeder does not hold a particular place of honor. Maybe weeding seems too slow or too primitive for our fast lives. But I know when I sit in a garden with my father's hand tool, that weeding is a good and a worthwhile way to spend one's life.

If You Could See What I See

If only we could practice seeing the real story beneath the outer presentation, the outer circumstances of our life.

One of my jobs in co-leading the weekend-long Opening the Heart Workshop is to read the "data sheets" that participants send us in the weeks leading up to the workshop. The four questions are: 1) Why are you coming to the workshop now in your life?; 2) What experiences are occurring in your life that you would like to address in the workshop?; 3) What major traumas have happened in your life?; 4) What major exultations have you experienced? Because the questions are optional, not everyone answers them, but many do. As the data sheets come in to me (mostly by e-mail), I sit with them, read them, "absorb" them, again and again, so that when participants enter the workshop space, as staff welcome them, I am putting faces to stories. I find the process of reviewing the stories very grounding and it helps me sincerely acknowledge people as they come into the room to sit in the circle. "Thank you for writing to us, Rita. You came a long way. Welcome…"

People look pleased that their words were read and I imagine that I see a bit of the terror in their faces that they walked in with, relax just a bit. As we sit waiting for the circle to fill, I look at the faces and remember that I have been doing this opening ritual now for 36 years. What I see as I look at our circle is that most people look alone and scared. I make up in my mind that some are thinking "What did I get myself into!?" I also make up in my mind that other people looking around the circle see 35-40 strangers, all trying to look comfortable and at ease. I will later refer to what's going on in this opening circle and say that as we look around into another's eyes and see difference, then we experience separation.

I do not experience this separation because I have already been privileged to be able to look behind the mask by knowing many peoples' stories. So, as I look across the circle at James, I see a tag line above his head that says "New father- wife just asked him for a divorce." When I look over at Carol, writing in her journal, the tag above her head is "Three children- newly diagnosed, inoperable cancer." Michael, off to my right, has a tag that says "Divorced twice- lonely."

I explain toward the end of the Friday night session that the reason I have come back to this workshop for so long is to see the miracle of the transformation of the circle from Friday night to Sunday morning when most will look into another's eyes, with the mask gone, and they will see what I saw Friday night: no difference. And when we see "no difference" in another's eyes, what we experience is compassion. We "get" the real story, the deeper story than the outer presentation we see on Friday night, and the one we, perhaps, usually see when we go to the post office to buy stamps or to the grocery to buy dinner.

I may tell the story about the father who brings his two young sons into a crowded waiting room of the pediatrician. The boys are disruptive. Most waiting patients go deeper into reading their magazine, but one older woman is visibly upset. Finally, she says to the father "Can't you control your boys!" The father looks embarassed and says "I'm so sorry. They lost their mother yesterday and I have not been able to console them." And so, in an instant, we "see" something different than what we thought we were seeing and our experience changes from judgment to sadness and compassion. There's an invitation, I think, to see beneath the mask when we can, and to even "make up" a tag, or story, that goes deeper than the one we think we see. Because when we can do that, it just becomes easier to practice lovingkindness with everyone. The Dalai Lama says that *when* we can do that, we create a more peaceful, loving world.

Two Loud Minutes of Silence

When we are able to see the wounds that others carry and recognize them as our own, we immediately experience compassion.

In a New Yorker magazine article by Michael Specter, he talked about Daniela Schiller and her father, Sigmund, who both had lived in Tel Aviv. Each year in Israel a siren announces two minutes of silence in remembrance of the Holocaust. Throughout the whole country, everything stops. Waiters stop waiting, bakers stop baking, people stop talking- except for Sigmund Schiller who is a concentration camp survivor, who goes about his day as if the siren had not sounded. His daughter, Daniela, recalls growing up asking her father: "Daddy, what happened in the war? Why do you never talk about it?" Her father never answered her, not a word, only silence. Silence is not precisely accurate. I think it was more like something darkly jagged locked away in a safety deposit box: safety because taking it out of the dark, locked place would be too overwhelming and painful.

Many years ago in my therapy practice, I saw a woman who had survived a small plane crash where more than half the passangers were killed. Four years later, after the crash, when I first saw her in therapy, she was still unable to remember anything that happened either months before or months after the accident. Something traumatic and scary had been locked away because it was too big to integrate it into her consciousness.

I currently work with a very brave woman, now in her early fifties, who was sexually abused by her father from the time she was seven until she was twelve. After six months of meeting with me, she shared one day about the abuse, afterward saying "I have never told this to anyone before." She told me about the abuse in a non-emotional, very matter-of-fact way. I waited patiently for her to share whatever she needed to. Then I said "Deanna, how does it feel to have shared this with me after keeping it inside for 45 years?" Even though there was silence for the next few minutes, a lot was happening. I thought of it as a "loud silence." She never looked directly at me. She bit her lip. One finger tapped on her knee. She was not breathing. She looked out the window at birds feeding at the feeder. Her finger tapped faster. She swallowed. Her eyes began to fill up. One tear fell down her cheek. I could not help but think of the ground trembling before a volcano erupts. Her body began to shake. She closed her eyes and a few more tears squeezed out down her cheek.

Then, as if a dam broke, she sobbed and she put her arms around herself. In the softest voice, barely audible, she said "I love my father." The tears continued for a long time and I thought of all the things we carry inside us, all the scars that hobble us- all the energy used in the most noble of efforts: to stay alive.

I also thought of Sigmund Schiller and how alone he had lived with his nightmares for so many decades. Sometimes we get lucky and we find a safe place to land, to lay the burden down, to no longer be afraid. What it must be like to wake up one morning and, consciously, not put on the body armor.

What I think I know is that many of us have not gone through a horror like a genocide or a childhood sexual abuse, or heartbreaking poverty or hunger. Still, I do believe that we all are human and have had our hearts break, our dreams dashed, our dear ones taken from us. Most of the time we don't get to see the scars that our brothers and sisters carry, but please assume that these wounds are most likely there, locked in a dark, secret place and that only love and kindness can help ease the pain.

Jon's Haikus

Watching the parade,
   better than marching in it,
   I think to myself.

It's never too late
   for redemption to heal hearts,
   I once heard it said.

Wounds we cannot see
   often scar the heart deeply:
   lovingkindness heals.

Opening the heart
   is a brave, holy journey:
   a breath, a home place.

Mulligans

I always loved the movie Groundhog Day: trying
again and again until we get it right.

I don't really consider myself a golfer, but I do play once or twice a year. Because I'm not an accomplished player, I'm not at risk for taking it too seriously and that allows me to enjoy the beauty of the course and being outdoors and to just have some fun with friends. I've learned from more accomplished partners about an interesting phenomenon called a *mulligan*. A mulligan, as I understand it, is basically a *do-over*. If I take a tee shot and top it into the pond, I can ask for a *mulligan*, and I tee it up again and, instead of hitting it into the pond, this time I can whack it into the woods. This, of course, logically, leads to the understanding that there are a limited number of times you can take a do-over. If you take the game half seriously, which occasionally I do, the bad shot can lead to self judgment, embarassment, discouragement (not to mention, clearly, what it feels like to screw up *two* shots in a row).

One of my all-time favorite movies is *Groundhog Day*. It's basically a love story but with a very clever twist. Bill Murray, as a reporter, goes to Punxsutawney to see if the groundhog shows his shadow on February 2nd. He gets to play the same day over and over and over again. He wakes up at 6am to his wake-up alarm: Sonny and Cher singing *I Got You Babe*. Over the course of each replayed day he keeps making stupid mistakes, awkward social gaffes, unkind words, one arrogance too many. But over time, as he continues his do-overs, he makes fewer errors, the rough edges get smoothed, the periods of thoughtlessness become more mindful. As he becomes more loving, he becomes more loveable and real, and Andie Macdowell falls totally in love with him. He could have packed his suitcase, left Punxsutawney and continued to bump into his self-created karma, but he chose the harder path, the true path for a man, i.e., trying to "get it right," of becoming a loving warrior.

Just about every one of the patients I see in my practice who has struggled with some kind of addiction, has followed the same "groundhog path" of do-overs. Not one of these people decides, after a thirty year addiction, to just start over and they do it, they get it right. They all "fail" many times before they have solid footing on a recovery path. But the GPS coordinates in my office call for a different language. In my office patients don't talk about gaffes or periods of thoughtlessness. They call them relapses. They lapse and then re-lapse. And, with each relapse comes, I think, the same kind of discouragement, shame, self consciousness (but bigger and deeper) that a semi-serious golfer experiences when they hit a bad tee shot. I bow to everyone who has the courage to risk trying again to get things right. I do find myself giving a deeper bow to the men who have this kind of courage because I just believe that it's harder in our culture for men to find the support and to give themselves the permission to do this kind of inner soul retrieval work.

I've heard it said that on a spiritual journey, being off the path is part of the path. I've also heard it put another way in regard to developing a mindfulness meditation practice: it doesn't matter how many times we go away. What matters is how many times we come back. So, may we all come back, again and again, from discouragement, loss and heartbreak until we hit a clean, straight, 200 yard drive right down the center of the fairway.

Big Love

"I meant what I said and I said what I meant, an elephant's
faithful one hundred percent!" ~ Dr. Suess

"Love is not love, which alters when it alteration finds..." Shakespeare

Now that I'm a grandfather ("Grumpy") and I find myself reading to my granddaughters the same great children's stories I was raised on, I have a whole new appreciation for these beautiful tales. I was recently very moved in reading Dr. Seuss' *Hortense Hatches an Egg*. This is a story about a manipulative, irresponsible bird who lays an egg but would prefer to vacation in warm weather rather than do the hard work of sitting in the nest, dry weather or wet, hot or freezing cold. The task for Maizie, then, is to find someone who will do the hard love for her. Enter Hortense the elephant.

Moved by Maizie's "story", he agrees to sit and hatch the egg. He makes Maizie a promise that he will do this: "I meant what I said and I said what I meant. An elephant's faithful one hundred percent!" Well, Old Hortense had no idea what he was getting himself into. First, an elephant sitting on a nest in a tree! Really? But Hortense would not back down. Then, as winter came, the weather turned freezing cold with sleet and snow and icicles hanging from Hortense's long trunk and ears. But he made a promise.... And he kept it month after lonely, hard month. I feel like this was Big Love. He made a noble promise to help someone and he hept his word.

I know, I know. Foolish, you might say. Naive! Easily manipulated! Maybe. But I believe that the authenticity, the Bigness of the deed is not measured by the outcome, but by the faithfulness of holding the love, the promise. Several years ago I saw a man in my therapy practice. He told me a very moving story about his marriage. This was a second marriage for him and it was the third marriage for his wife. He told me that he knew when he married "Chloe" that she had a history of having affairs. Sure enough, in his four year marriage, Chloe was having a second affair since marrying my patient, Aaron. When he confronted her with the affair, she boldly told him that she would not end it.

Aaron told me that he deeply loved Chloe and, in spite of how hurt and upset he was, he would not leave her. And so, the affair continued for months while he waited. He did not run. He told me that he and Chloe, several weeks prior to our therapy session, went to see the movie *Philomena*. After the movie, he noticed that she was unusually quiet and withdrawn. As they sat in a private, quiet restaurant, she looked at him and her eyes filled up. Then she sobbed into her cloth napkin. He had no idea what this was all about until she was able to catch her breath and she explained that the movie had connected her to a deep truth about herself, of which she had never been aware. She told Aaron that she now understood why she'd had so many affairs and, unconsciously, tried to push every man in her life into leaving her. When she was six, her father left the family and she never saw him again. She realized that she had put men in the same position of forcing them to abandon her the way her father had. She now knew that what she had always really wanted was a man who wouldn't run. She acknowledged how she had hurt Aaron and she asked for his forgiveness.

It actually doesn't matter whether this ended up having a happy ever after ending. I think what matters is that his Big Love allowed her to let go of something that had weighed her down for over half a century. Again, you might say, what kind of fool would "put up" with ongoing disrespect from his wife. I don't know how to answer that except to say the kind of fool capable of holding a very rare and healing love.

Inner Serenity Is for Losers

Who of us has the courage to be loving instead of right?

I have been seeing "Maria" in my therapy practice for about four years. She has been grieving her forty year marriage to Luis for a long time. They raised two children and went through the ups and downs that most couples in long term relationships go through. Though Maria has been grieving her marriage, I should make clear that they are still married. The thing that Maria told me that was so poignant about their marriage is that every night, before going to bed, they would kiss and tell each other "I love you." They did this every night, through the ups and downs- until they didn't.

About 20 years ago, Luis' mood started to change. He became volatile and reactive. When Maria would remark to him that he "forgot" to kiss her and say "I love you" at night, Luis would get angry and defensive and would insist that he had not forgotten. Maria noticed that he tended to brood and would become depressed with no obvious reason. This "change of personality," as she called it, not only remained over time, it got worse. He frequently became suspicious of her normal nights out with friends. He started to become belligerant and one night he pushed her and blocked her from leaving the house.

Luis did accept her plea to see his doctor and he agreed to antidepressant medication and therapy, but his mental status continued to deteriorate, as did their marriage. Maria's heart was broken. She had somehow lost the love of her life right before her eyes and he kept drifting further away despite her efforts to bring him in from the cold, back to the home they'd known together for so long.

When she found out about his affair, she was angry and crushed and he vehemently denied it and got angrier and more threatening. When she first came to see me, it was to help her cope with the heartbreaking loss she could not change: Luis had left her for the dark world of mental illness. Maria worked bravely to learn how to breathe and remain calm when Luis became reactive. It is a hard and courageous thing to keep trying to be kind when hard winds blow. I always supported her to be clear about not accepting abusive or threatening behavior and she got into the habit of having an overnight bag packed and a dear friend available when the storms got too strong.

Maria did learn how to remain calm, even to continue to practice lovingkindness at the times his mental and physical condition worsened. Maria did a lot of grief work to mourn her losses. For many reasons, she decided to stay in the

marriage, not the least of which was that she felt she could not abandon him in his deeply compromised condition. Luis' condition did not improve but Maria noted that he did become softer, less belligerent. And then one night something happened that knocked her way off balance: he kissed her before bedtime and told her he loved her. She did not know what to say or do. She said to me "Jon, I have practiced letting go for so many years now. Though my heart is still broken and I still grieve, I have found some serenity. How do I respond when he says, 'I love you'?"

We talked for a long time. She knew there was no way to revive the marriage and she could never go back. Maria decided to do an amazing thing: she chose to continue to practice lovingkindness and, in response to his "I love you," she began to smile and say "I love you too." She continued to practice watching the parade instead of marching in it. She continued to keep letting go of what she couldn't control. The Buddhists say that we suffer when we hold on to something that has to leave us. This is why, I think, that inner serenity is only for those who are brave enough to keep letting go of all the things we are all bound to lose as human beings.

Never Too Late

Aim high, and when we fall, just show up again tomorrow.

Since I'm a big Red Sox fan, it's not surprising that I was recently watching them play a night game against the Orioles. When they fell behind 5-0, I'd seen enough and went to bed. In the morning, I read about the Sox' thrilling come from behind win in the last three innings and I said to myself, once again, "It's never too late."

Actually, it's that phrase and the belief behind it, that determines what movies I watch and how I do my lifelong work as a psychologist in my therapy practice. The films that are most deeply moving for me are the ones about redemption, where the characters have been roughed up by life's hard times and, as a result, they've become hard or mean, but some small event or a meeting or a divine descension of grace, transforms the heart and leads to a life of deeper wisdom or kindness. This transformation is what I witness every time I lead an Opening the Heart weekend workshop. And it's the same transformation I see so often in my therapy practice. It's never too late. No one knows our name until our last breath goes out.

But, honestly, I've come to admit that, maybe, sometimes, it *is* too late. It's early spring and I'm always excited about putting new plantings in the earth in the serenity garden on the deck outside my office window. I feel like a wiser planter than I was when I first started the garden three years ago. By that I mean that I know what plants will bloom all summer, which will survive the heat, which will be back next spring. But if I don't choose well now, then come August and September. It really will be too late to alter the outcome of the garden.

I've mentioned in a previous essay a man in my practice in his mid sixties who was diagnosed with inoperable pancreatic cancer and I wrote how much I admired his efforts to try to "get some things right" before his life was over. I see another woman who is 81 who also has inoperable cancer. She speaks bitterly about her family with whom she has had little contact over many years. She decided to write letters to her children and grandchildren to try to bring closure for herself. She has not seen any of her grandchildren in over three years. She asked for my help regarding what to say in the letters.

If I'm honest, which I was not with her, there was a part of me that shook my inner head and said silently "It really is too late to make a difference in how this woman's life would play out." Who knows, who am I to say, maybe she could write how sorry she was that she had chosen to harden her heart for so long. Maybe she could wish that her children and grandchildren never make the same mistake she made- that it was not too late for them. Maybe she could tell them that she forgave them for any ways, intentionally or not, that they hurt her. And maybe she could ask them for forgiveness and tell them that she loved them. So, maybe, it was not too late for her to get some things "right" before her life came to an end.

And what about Big Mistakes that we may have made that cost people their dignity, their homes, even their lives? I don't know the answers to these questions. I really don't know if sometimes, maybe, it is too late. I just think that all we imperfect beings can ever do is to aim high, do our best, take responsibility when we fail and then show up again the next day. Maybe this does come back, once again, to practicing self kindness and doing the hardest forgiving of all- of ourselves.

On Loan

Nothing is ever really ours. Be a good shepherd while we have it.

"No one brings a rental car to a car wash." ~ Confucius 470 B.C.

In Naomi Shihab Nye's poem *Kindness*, she says "Before we can know kindness as the deepest thing inside, we must lose things." Why? How does that work that we have to lose things before kindness becomes a part of us? The answer: I don't know! But when I think of the times that I've lost things and been brought to my knees with grief, those are the times when I am cracked open and feel a larger connection to all people. Because the truth is that each of us will lose everything we think we own. I say 'think' because I believe that everything we 'have' has only been loaned to us.

I find myself often looking around my home for things to give away or get rid of. Now that our kids are married with lives of their own, I go to the basement and see boxes of things: 25-pound bags of clay that hardened into bricks long before the turn of the century. I see a microwave that only works when you push the odd numbers (except for the '7'). And the books! Hundreds of books that I loved but can't seem to let go of even though I've read them all at least once. Classical records I know I will never play again- especially since I don't have a working record player. (Do my kids even know what a "record" is?) But these things were all important to me at one time, and now I'm looking to get rid of them- "downsizing" is the word, I think, we older people use. Making room for... what? Maybe what we should have made room for a lot sooner.

Krishna Das is a seeker and a beautiful chanter who tells the story of going to India to see his guru,Neem Karoli Baba. When he stood before him, Das' guru told him to meditate. Das winced and said "How?" Baba said "Like Christ!" Das said "Jesus!" Baba closed his eyes and went inside and after just a few minutes, a tear rolled down his cheek. He opened his eyes, looked at Das and said "That is how Christ meditates."

About twenty years ago I was at a meditation retreat and I had a profound experience. Breathing in patience, breathing out warmth. I went very deep and I began to let go of everything I owned. Consciously feeling it, remembering, then letting it go. When I was done with the things, I started with relationships - all of them. I admit, it was hard to keep breathing, but I did. Tears fell, until nothing was left except my breath. Then I counted down each breath until the last one. Empty space....

Nothing, I think, is really ours. We only have them on loan for a very little time. That's a good thing, maybe. Rationalization? Probably, but, honestly, the finiteness of what we've been given allows us to breathe in the sweetness of it when we can be calm, and then allow our heart to break when we have to give it back to the Owner.

Praying in the Circle

Sitting in a circle for the purpose of healing can be a holy experience.

A few years ago, I took an early morning walk east along Horseneck Beach in Westport. I was heading toward a nature preserve at the end of the beach. As I walked, I watched the ospreys hunting for fish while the terns hovered and then dove for a small herring. If you had asked me why I had gotten up so early or what I was looking for on that walk, I doubt I could have told you- but I know now what it was. I was looking for serenity and quiet. I was looking for a house of prayer. And I found it.

As I crossed the small island, I took in the beauty: ocean, early morning, sun reaching the top of the tree line, scrub oak, the delicate smell of wild primrose in bloom. I was heading toward the dunes and the ocean. As I ascended up the dune, I could see more and more of the ocean. As I reached the top of the dune and began the descent, I froze. My heart stopped and the breath went out of me. There on the beach were 10 great blue herons, all facing the offshore wind coming from the ocean. They were roughly arranged in a skewed circle. They must have been praying because this was a holy place I had come to. I know in some religions you need at least 10 people to make a congregation for the prayer service to happen. I just watched, and then, silently, one of them said "Amen", and they all took off together, flying over the water.

Without any signal or word, they all turned right and flew right over me and I could hear the "whoosh" of their great wings. The "whoosh", even then, I remember as the sound one's blood makes when it pumps back into the heart. When we are fully inside a moment of awe, the blood pumps, the senses come fully awake, time dissolves.

Some time ago, I wrote a book with my son called *Sitting in the Circle*. It's a series of essays about the inspiration I've received from my patients in my therapy office and from the work that participants do at a weekend-long Opening the Heart workshop. There is something archetypal and powerful about sitting in a circle at the beginning of each workshop session, in a community of brothers and sisters who have come together for the purpose of healing emotional wounds.

The more I thought about it this past year, the more I realized that much more than sitting happens in the circle. For me it is a holy pilgrimage. It is a kind of prayer service that happens in the circle. The service starts with the yearning.

I call it "showing up." There's a prayer that says "With all my heart have I gone out to seek You, and in the going out, found You coming toward me." The yearning is the core of the answer to the call. It is the echo of the prayer for yearning. So in doing the work during a workshop, in making the descent and the ascent, we bring the passion for healing, the cry of the heart, the scream, the pounding of a pillow, the tear.

I saw one woman at a workshop looking into her partner's eyes across from her, and for the first time since her husband died suddenly in their bed seven years ago, she cried. And the whoosh of the heart revived her back from a seven year paralysis. I saw a man, again in lines work, kill a priest who had sexually abused this man for four years when he was a little boy. And whoosh, blood flowed to parts of the body that had been dead for decades.

A good, juicy prayer service brings us home, to a place where there's more peace and serenity, more compassion and self love. This kind of big transformation happens again and again within a sacred circle of people who are praying as if their life depends on it. Because, honestly, it does.

Missing the Trops

How to stop a stream of negative thoughts
to avoid reacting from a triggered place.

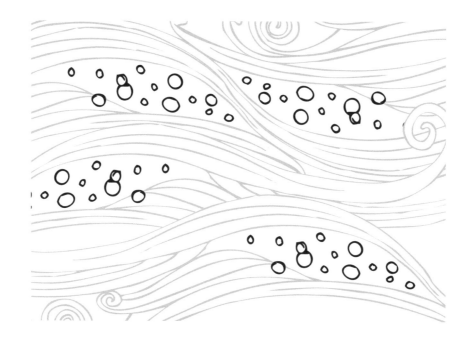

In Fenway Park there's a men's room right across from the ramp leading out into the stands near home plate. The men's room is diagonally across from the hot pretzels ($5, with mustard) and the sausage sandwiches with onions and peppers ($7.50). This particular men's room has 74 urinals with no partitions. Yes, as a matter of fact, I *did* count them, while I was waiting in line to use one. That's right, every single one was taken. I know this may be more information than you needed on men's rooms, but, be patient- I am aiming higher. So, I took my turn, and the guy on my left turns to me and says "trops". I was so startled at this breach of etiquette, I could only say "What!?", because, in fact, I had no idea what he was communicating by "trops". He repeated: "trops". Still shaken and trying to collect myself and wanting to end this unwanted exchange, I said "Yup!"

He continued: "The 'troughs'- I miss the troughs they used to have here." Inside, I tried to breathe and remind myself that this whole unpleasant exchange would be over in a whiz, but I had to consciously keep from calling an attendant to come and take away the man at urinal #54. In other words, I'd been triggered.... By what, I asked myself.

Well, for one, men's public urinal etiquette has been established for thousands of years. You stand in front of the urinal. You may look down or straight ahead, but never to the left or right. And you never, ever, speak to anyone while urinating. I don't know that these rules have ever been written down and I do not find anything on an internet search of "Men's public urinal etiquette." Nonetheless, the understanding of these rules, I believe, goes back to the Babylonians who had porcelain troughs and, at least for the patrician class, there would have been a designated place to stand at the trough. In other words, there's a lot of weight behind these expectations of how to behave under these circumstances....

Okay, so maybe the triggering was also connected to a bit of homophobia. Phobia means fear, and I think it is fear that is at the root of almost all triggered behavior. What I say to my patients in my office in regard to behavior in relationships is that there are two rules: 1) Never speak or act from a reactive, triggered place because there will never, ever, be a good harvest; 2) See Rule #1.

So *how* do you not react from a triggered place? It is from this triggered place that we are absolutely convinced of the 'rightness' of our position. The word 'rightness' is very close, etymologically, to the word 'righteousness'. One important thing I have tried to practice for many years is that when I recognize the physiological signs of triggering, or 'an arrow going in', I try to breathe. When I feel startled, surprised, fearful, angry, hurt, these feelings will be experienced in the body, and one response to those feelings is to gasp, or stop breathing. When I am able to take a breath, I increase my chances of being able to take a second breath. And if I can do that, then I am putting some distance between the stimulus and the response. And with that distance, comes an increased possibility of making a conscious response, rather than a reflexive one.

So, what this meant on that night at Fenway was that, instead of saying something hostile or angry, or making a scene by calling for an attendant, I could breathe, zip up and leave- a reasonable stream of thought, yes?

Walking on the Moon

We are incredibly resourceful beings in creating ways to survive and heal.

If you're fifty or older, there are certain events in history that you're likely to remember vividly. When I was once asked "Where were you, Jon, when President Kennedy was killed?", I remembered walking out of the library at Brandeis University on Friday afternoon, November 22nd 1963, when I heard the news. I also remember being in the living room of my host family in London on July 20th 1969, watching Neil Armstrong taking the first steps on the moon. Even though the black and white film was grainy and jumpy, I remember thinking "What a magical moment!" I was twenty three years old on the frontier of my young life watching men on the frontier of space exploration jumping around on the moon like kids on a playground. Watching those footsteps in the moon dust was etched in my memory forever.

I have been seeing Anna in my therapy practice for over nine years. She is in her mid fifties now, petite and really bright and tremendously brave. Before I knew better, she would lead me into deep conversations like "What is love?" I say "before I knew better" because I would blunder in to answer, thinking it was a wise and solid response, and within minutes, she would peel back the easy answers, always going deeper until I learned to listen rather than speak. She didn't set a "trap" or anything like that. She was always sincere, thoughtful and earnest about digging for truth. She is always a force.

Anna had ten brothers and sisters and each and every one of them, including Anna, were sexually abused by their father for many years growing up. Anna was the only one who "made it out alive." Some of the others committed suicide, most had drug and alcohol addictions. None of them, except Anna, had a loving partner, family or community. She has asked me, a number of times, "Why did I make it out, Jon?" I had learned my lessons with Anna. I had to gently listen to where her question would lead her.

She talked about the next door neighbors, the family where she was loved and where, sometimes, she found safe refuge. The family never knew the real story. Anna talked about this family as, perhaps, why she made it out. And she also talked about a God-given faith and she also talked about walking on the moon. Anna had a mobile hanging above her bed. It had all the planets including earth and our moon. She remembered that when she heard his footsteps coming down the hall, coming to "pay a visit," she would visit the rings of Saturn but, especially, she would go to the moon and

walk and play in that magical place. She had to remember things in great detail. She remembers the breathtaking view of earth, the beautiful shining stars in the vast darkness and the peace and silence and safety of walking on the moon. She would often stay long after the "visit" was over. With tears in her eyes, Anna said "I walked on the moon long before Neil Armstrong and Buzz Aldrin."

In therapy, Anna found a way to become more whole than she had ever been in her life. She had, amazingly, found a way to "make it out" by learning when (and with whom) to make a descent and go after the answers to her deep questions- her answers. And she also knew when, in her life, to fly up and survive by walking on the moon.... Sleep, Anna, sleep. There's a morning to come....

Sitting With the Shattered Heart

When sitting with someone whose heart has been shattered,
one learns to sit quietly, respectfully and compassionately.

How does one sit with someone who has a shattered heart? I think the simple answer is: respectfully and compassionately. The real answer, though, is hardly simple. This kind of 'being' with someone who has experienced bone-numbing loss and life-draining defeat sometimes means going down into the descent yourself to help someone put their skin back on and to open a space for their soul to come back to their body.

As well as I can figure it, over the course of 36 years of helping to lead the Opening the Heart workshop, I have facilitated hundreds of Healing Circles. The Healing Circle is a small group exercise of about six participants who, in Leonard Cohen's words, come to "gather around the brokenness" of each brother or sister in turn as they lay on a mat and are 'loved through' a wound that maybe they have carried for decades. It's important to know the context of this exercise within the whole workshop. I call Healing Circles "the last stop before the highway." In other words, it comes at the end of a day-long descent of cathartic emotional release work, the final act of 'emptying the cup', before it is refilled in the second part of the workshop.

They say when you have a very intense experience, you remember it as if it were happening in slow motion, I think because you are totally in the moment to everything that unfolds. I remember in very fine detail when Cindy took her place on the mat, with those around her laying hands gently on her as she breathed. Seven years before the workshop, she woke one morning and found her husband next to her not breathing. They had been married three years and Cindy was five months pregnant. She was devastated and lost without her husband and she gave birth four months later to a beautiful baby boy. When her baby was seven months old, he died of SIDS and Cindy began a period of paralysis and grief that was unmovable. I watched Cindy as she went through the first part of the workshop. I never saw her cry or express any feeling at all.

As she lay on the mat, I remember feeling broken-hearted for her. I lay by her head, prayed, and waited with her. Staying quiet and just being with her was hard. I did not want to try to 'make something happen' for her. But I remember, after what was a very long few minutes, asking her if she was willing to 'try something'. Though she didn't know what this "something" was, she said "Yes." I helped her sit up and asked her to pick two others in the circle to be her husband and infant son. She closed her eyes tight, but opened them and picked two people who sat in front of her. With eyes closed again, I asked her to bring into sharp focus the faces of her lost loved ones and then asked her to open her eyes and see those loved ones sitting before her. Then I asked her to speak to them.

It took her a while to find the words but she told them about her shattered heart, about her grief. She spoke of the pain of missing them, and then something happened that surprised me. She told them of how ashamed she felt for not being able to move on with her life as she knew they would want her to. And as she looked into their eyes, one tear came down her cheek but she choked back the weeping that was there.

I wish I could say that this experience was deeper and more healing for her, but I realized that that one tear had caused her heart to break- not break down, but break open. At the very end of the workshop, as each person had a chance to share their workshop experience with the whole group, Cindy said "I am not in a healed or happy place, but I now know what I have to do to start living again". This was more than enough for me, and I hope her, to start putting her skin back on and to begin to let her soul return to her body. I believe it's never too late for the miracle of healing to happen.

Banpop

To be able to give loving nurturance, without ever having received it, is an amazing achievement.

"We all have two lives. The second one starts when we realize the first one ends." ~ A patient of mine

I used to see Sam in my therapy practice once a week for a long time. Now he calls me once every year or two, leaving me a message that he just wants to "check in and shoot the shit." Sam came in with his five year old granddaughter, Louisa. He introduced me as a friend and he led her into my office with a loving, reassuring presence. He asked her to tell me what they were going to do that day. Louisa, cute as a precious button, put her finger to her mouth, looked up at the ceiling and said slowly "Mu-se-um, and the ocean and go for a hike." Sam smiled again and said to me "Not only pretty, but very smart!" He spoke to her in an adult voice and treated her with constant love and respect. He reassured her that he wanted to talk with me for a while and that they would go whenever she wanted. She smiled and said "Thank you Banpop." Sam explained that when Louisa was born, his son asked Sam what he wanted to be called when this new Being of Light was old enough to talk. He told his son "Let her choose my name." So when she was about two, she started calling him 'Banpop', and it stuck.

Sam brought me up to date on his life. His son, once in big trouble with drugs, was now clean for four years, was working, and was in a solid relationship. Sam's own relationship of twelve years was a hard one and he said, "It may be that we go our own ways..... I've learned, from you, that I can only do what I can do. I can only save myself."

Sam is about my age, in his late 60's. He grew up in a very physically abusive home, beaten frequently by a father who was alcoholic and had never had a chance to learn how to be a loving father. Sam became a marine at eighteen and went to Vietnam for three tours where he saw very bad things that, still, at times, haunt him. He is in great shape, handsome, active and he has bright eyes and a warm smile.

He looked at Louisa, then back at me and said "You know, Jon, the worst thing that can happen to a person is for them to lose their childhood." I said "Sam, I am so proud of you for being able to give something you never got." I asked if I could read him a poem by Mary Oliver called The Journey. He smiled.

"One day you finally knew what you had to do, and began, though the voices kept shouting their bad advice... 'Mend my life!' But you didn't stop... though it was a wild night and the road full of fallen branches, you left the voices behind... determined to do the only thing you could do- determined to save the only life you could save."

Tears were falling down Sam's face. Louisa looked at him and said "Why are you crying Banpop?" "Sometimes people cry because they're happy, Honey."

I have come to understand that Sam's "check-ins" are about telling me that he has left those voices behind and now lives in a more loving and kinder way that has changed family tradition. He can leave a different legacy than the one he received. Oh, and I do believe he also comes for the hug before he goes back out into the world.

Deep Listening

To practice deep listening is a rare thing and a healing gift.

Jack Kornfield is a clinical psychologist, a Buddhist monk and a high school friend. In his book *A Lamp in the Darkness*, he tells a poignant story that awakened something deep in me. He tells us about Dr. Richard Seltzer, a Yale surgeon, who had decided to attend grand rounds one day because of a special visit by a visiting foreign physician. The doctor was Yeshi Dhonden, the Dalai Lama's personal physician, who would be meeting with a patient chosen by the hospital staff in order to make a diagnosis and to discuss the case with the other attending whitecoats.

Dr. Seltzer learned that before grand rounds, Yeshi Dhonden had bathed, fasted and prayed and then showed up exactly on time at 6am in the patient's room. His head was shaved and he wore a golden saffron robe. He approached her slowly and reverently, a woman in her early fifties, and he looked at her for a long time. He also, to Dr. Seltzer, seemed to be looking above her body. Finally, he came to her side and gently raised her wrist with both his hands. As he felt for her pulse, he bent over her, "like a golden eagle", holding her wrist in his hands without moving, for a full half hour. The patient raised her head off her pillow several times to look at him, then rested her head back. Dr. Seltzer noted, to himself, that on seeing this scene unfold, he had an awareness of having palpated a thousand pulses, but not really had an awareness of even one. Dr. Seltzer reflected that he felt jealous: not of Yeshi Dhonden, and his powerful presence, but of the patient- to be so deeply listened to and received. When Yeshi Dhonden was done, he gently rested her wrist back on her stomach and backed away toward the door, never turning his back on her. As he was about to leave, the patient raised her head, touched the wrist he had held, and said "Thank you Doctor." Yeshi Dhonden smiled and left, never having spoken one word.

In the conference room, through his interpreter, this skilled healer spoke in poetic terms about a great wind and rushing waters that had had their effect on the patient long before she was born. The head of grand rounds asked what was the diagnosis. Yeshi said "congenital heart failure." The patient had little time left to live. A reverant quiet filled the room.

The reason the story touched me so deeply was that I know this kind of deep listening when the Quiet comes. It is exactly this kind of listening that we aim to bring to any of our brothers or sisters, whether they are patients in a therapy office, or people selling us bread or stamps. I thought, though, specifically about the love and safety set up at an Opening the Heart workshop. Especially, it called to mind each person lying on a mat surrounded by six caring brothers and sisters who are laying gentle hands on this soul in the middle and then, there is a staff person, a facilitator, who sits by the person's head, and first silently prays for healing to enter the circle. It is always a transformative experience to help create this cocoon of safety for deep listening to happen. There is an awareness that the healing that happens occurs not because of a change in life circumstances for that person, but because they have been brave enough to offer their tender heart to be seen and received by others. The healing happens because they have been truly heard.

I believe that there are two things that allow this kind of transformational change for a person: 1) their willingness to have their heart break, not break down but break open and 2) the intention and skillful dedicated practice of listening to pulses, to the deeper experience of a soul than just the mask or external presentation they give us. The other name for this listening to what is beneath the body armor is Love.

If Words Could Kill

Before speaking: Is it true? Is it kind? Is it necessary?

I had not seen Richard in my therapy office for over three years. He called, in tears, asking to see me that afternoon. When he came in, his eyes were red and he looked like he had not slept in a long time. I asked him to talk to me. He told me that four nights ago he had said an early good night to his wife of twenty years who had not felt well in the early evening. He sat by her bedside, held her hand and she said she was sure she would be all right in the morning. They talked a while, remembering sweet memories of their early time together. They laughed and cried a bit, kissed good night and he turned out the light.

Richard, in his early fifties, told me that in the morning, he found his wife not breathing and cold to the touch. He was devastated. But what he could not get out of his mind was that four days earlier, he and his wife had had a bad argument, and in a moment of frustration and rage, he said to her "I wish you were dead! And the sooner the better!" Even though the autopsy revealed that she had died of a massive heart attack (and there was a family history of heart disease), he was absolutely convinced that it was his hard words that had cut deeply and broken her heart. He told me that he and his wife had had a good and loving marriage, but, like all couples, they'd had dark times, arguments, harsh words, but he'd never, ever before, wished her dead.

Though I really wanted to reassure him, I found myself doubting and I actually did a search on whether, in fact, one could die of a broken heart. The answer, I learned, was that yes, people *did* die of a broken heart. I read case after case of couples in close long term relationships, where one partner died within hours or days of losing their "other half". But, these examples were different from a partner in a relationship dying from cruel or abusive words. Yet, I also remembered all the people I had seen in my office who still, decades later, remembered the crippling words delivered by an unskillful parent or family member- words that, when repeated over long periods of time, may not "kill", but *did* leave people wounded, scarred, broken.

So I think, how ironic that the coin of trade in my professional and personal life is a practice of mindful speech-attempting to use words that heal wounds caused by hurtful speech. Buddhism's concept of Right Speech consists of answering three questions: 1) Is it true?; 2) Is it kind?; 3) Is it necessary? I believe that we, literally, create who we are by the words we choose to use with others. It is loving words, aligned with a loving heart, that save lives. Kabir, a 15th century Sufi poet said "Love cuts a lot of arguments short." Love cuts right through the rightness or wrongness of a position and it heals.

A patient, a woman racked by a lifetime of shame over her body image and her eating disorder married a man who was quite judgmental of her weight until he decided to go to therapy himself to try to "get some things right." One night he woke and walked downstairs to find his wife sitting in the dark with an empty ice cream carton on the coffee table. She was weeping. He came over to her, put a hand on her shoulder, held her and said "I love you." Her shame dissolved in the presence of his kindness and love.

So, I told Richard what I believed: that his wife had died of a major coronary because her time had come and that his harsh words contributed *not at all* to her death. I also told him that he now had an opportunity to be a better, more mindful, chooser of the words he used with others in his life.

Letter From the Back Ward

Attempting to poke fun at myself and my own struggles to quiet a busy, negative mind.

This is a sad story. It's about the undoing of a man- a clinical psychologist in private practice for many years who was also a former Chief of Mental Health Services for a prominent large medical group services provider. And he also has served as a senior leader of the Opening the Heart workshop for 36 years.... Yes, it is my story.

For years in my private practice I tried to help people find their way home by teaching mindfulness meditation practice and how to acquire skillful means to tolerate and work beyond suffering, stress and trauma. I was devoted to my own practice of using mindfulness in order to attempt to "walk the walk" before presuming to help someone else find their way home.... Until the woodchucks came.

We lived in a rural area in a very old central chimney cape with a beehive oven, wide floor boards and ten beautiful acres of woods and organically farmed gardens. Since we love the outdoors, and since this was our first home, we had great dreams and expectations. We bought a 24 cubic foot freezer, ten chickens and a rooster, bought *Ten Acres and Independence* and began to till and plant a huge garden: everything from asparagus, blueberries, brussels sprouts, corn, tomatoes, peppers- everything. We came to realize there were many things we did not know- like that the authors of *Ten Acres and Independence* did not have full time jobs; like you never, ever, name the chickens that you will one day sit down to dine on. Also we did not know that woodchucks were omnipresent and omnivorous.

When we first saw them eating our garden, yes, it was unsettling, but I practiced slow deep breathing, calmly walked to the garden to shoo them away, embracing a practice of wishing love to all sentient beings. Within several weeks the ugly transformation began to take place. I bought a Have-A-Heart trap and got very excited the first morning to see from my bedroom window that the trap had been tripped and something was inside the trap. My next door neighbor, during the night, had put his son's teddy bear inside the trap and I almost had a good-hearted laugh with him when I returned the stuffed bear. From traps, I went to gas bombs and then to a rifle, with no success.

I began to have fantasies of catching a woodchuck and placing a boom box next to the cage, playing non-stop Barry Manilow songs until the whole family agreed to leave. Yes, the undoing was happening. I planted marigolds next to remaining crops because my research said woodchucks hated marigolds. They don't! The marigolds were eaten too. I really did try to watch the rage and not go marching in the parade.

Then one early evening we were sitting in the solarium which looked out on the garden when the whole family of woodchucks walked by outside. The father stopped, looked in directly at me and started making funny faces at me. My wife says this never happened, but I know it did. It became harder and harder to maintain a balanced perspective. I breathed, I meditated, I prayed and I raged....

I am writing this now from the back ward of the State Hospital. They say I am getting better. I have earned passes to go home on weekends, but only during winter months when woodchucks are in hibernation. Friends come to visit and they have an accepting, compassionate way of holding hope for my recovery. I do feel less angry but, since my treatment is about truth telling, I do admit that sometimes, when the attendant comes with his medication tray, I swear I see whiskers under his nose, and the back of his pants really do look like they have a tail packed inside.

Hey You!

An invitation to see deeper truth than what external circumstances present.

It was a Saturday morning at an Opening the Heart workshop just as participants were entering the room from breakfast. Friday night had been a beautiful and poignant beginning of the weekend journey at Kripalu and very few of the participants had ever been to this magical place before. So, as participants came into the workshop space Saturday morning, most began to find their way to a backjack in the circle. One woman, though, came over to me and said "Jon, I'd like to tell you an interesting story." I sat down and listened.

She told me that she'd never been to Kripalu before and when she came into the cafeteria hall for breakfast, she paused and just looked around to "take in the scene." She said she was "taken aback" to notice how solemn and unfriendly the whole atmosphere was. "Here were 250 people sitting in one space and I didn't see one person talking to anyone else! It was so depressing and unwelcoming!" She told me that as she continued to look around, she noticed the signs indicating two separate food lines for "vegetarian" and "nonvegetarian", and then she saw the sign that said "Breakfast is a silent meal."

She smiled as she continued to explain to me that when she saw that sign, she took in a deep breath of appreciation and gratitude. She told me that it was so beautiful to witness the whole room in a silent honoring of the invitation to stop the normal social distractions, to go inside and become more mindful of the practice of eating a beautifully prepared, healthy meal. She said that she noticed some people sitting with a smile or with their eyes closed, chewing food prepared and presented with love. Her eyes twinkled as she said "It was so awesome to take this in. The whole room was like one silent, holy prayer!"

Some weeks ago a favorite patient in my office began the session by telling me a story of what happened to her as she ended her day at a stressful and unhappy job. She walked out of the building into the parking lot. As she approached her car, she saw something under the windshield of her car. "I was so angry. At first, I thought it was a parking ticket. As I got closer, I saw that it was not a ticket, but a handwritten note." She said she noticed a fleeting feeling of relief that it wasn't a ticket, but then she saw the relief give way to a deep annoyance that someone would disrespect her private property and have the nerve to write her "some insulting note about parking five inches over the parking lane stripe!"

She took the note from the windshield and noticed the two words written there: "Hey you!" She felt her body tighten, and, as she unfolded it, she read the rest of the message: "You are here to evolve your consciousness and to learn how to grow more love in your life. Everything is unfolding exactly as it should." She told me that she read it again, took a deep breath and smiled. "My whole day, actually, my whole week changed and I took the challenge seriously of going through each day choosing to be a little kinder and more loving to whomever I met."

What struck me about both of these stories was that nothing externally had changed at all. But what made all the difference was the internal change of how these two women chose to see the external circumstances of their lives. Aldous Huxley once wrote that "It is not the external circumstances of our lives that matter. It is our attitude about those circumstances that makes all the difference." I thought, once again, that a lot of amazing things happen when we slow down, breathe and pay attention.

Seeing the Face of God

An interesting and, I think, provocative glimpse at some of the new research on psychedelics.

When I think of the experience that derives from participation in an Opening the Heart workshop, I think of what people say in the final sharing circle at the end of the weekend. Many times, with tears in their eyes, they speak about feeling joy, coming alive, feeling unrestrained love for others. Often they will say the workshop was the most powerful experience they'd ever had. What has been even more poignant is when someone, years later, comes over to me, hugs me and says that the workshop "changed my life".

This, of course, does not happen to every participant, but it does happen consistently enough over 36 years that it leaves me wondering exactly what has happened in one short weekend that caused such profound change for so many. I think about the loving, safe environment that allows people to go deep and release years of pain and suffering, depression, deep loss, even fear of death. There is the heart-opening experience of sharing that lonely grief with others, and realizing that we all have carried these wounds. I think about the skilled, experienced leaders who know the landscape of emotional healing and the transformative journey from fear to love. I think about how music, singing, and chanting are transformative, and I think they are a part of what wakes us up.

I had written a while ago about the power of miracles, or what my mentor, Abraham Maslow, called peak experiences. He said these experiences are not just extremely life-affirming events that break open the heart, but they are, themselves, life-changing experiences. One cannot walk away from a miracle and expect to be the same again. So all the components I mention above are a part of what changes us, but also, what changes in us is perspective. We see with Beginner's Eyes.

In 2006 a man named Roland Griffiths published a study in "Psychopharmacology" titled "Psilocybin Can Occasion Mystical-Type Experiences Having Substantial and Sustained Personal Meaning and Spiritual Significance." Because he had a track record as a serious and meticulous researcher, others became interested in re-opening the research on psychedelics that was shut down in 1970. In the past fifteen years, well-designed double blind studies at NYU, Johns Hopkins, UCLA and the College of London have started to look at how these molecules could effect addictions like smoking and alcoholism; anxiety and depression; and cancer and end of life experience. The goal of many of these studies was to "make the direct experience of the sacred more available to more people." I think this quote captures the essence of the Opening the Heart workshop.

In 2010 a 54 year old television news editor, Patrick Mettes, was diagnosed with bile duct cancer. He was going through heavy chemotherapy and was scared of losing everything he loved, as well as facing his own death. He was accepted to an NYU clinical trial of psychedelics. Because he was a journalist, he wrote about his day-long trial. Initially, he wrote that he felt intense fear and anxiety. Soon he was crying and having a "rebirthing" experience. Midway through his trip he remembered saying "OK, we can all punch out now. I get it." He wrote that he realized that love was the only purpose of life. He said he was being told on his trip that his cancer was "no big deal." He wrote "Oh God, it all makes sense now, so simple and beautiful."

Patrick lived for another seventeen months. His wife said that during those months, he was able to live in the present, to be joyful, enjoy a sandwich and to be more serene and at peace. She reported that he had told her he had seen "the face of God", and that he had been the happiest he had ever been in his life.

There's Really an App for That?

When we pay attention to the present moment, we're better able to face the fear and anxiety about the past.

A friend shared this story that resonated deeply with me. A man with a significant history of anger problems began seeing a therapist who recommended that the man attend an eight week mindfulness course to more effectively deal with the anger. "Joe" was six weeks into the course when he found himself one day in a long checkout line at the grocery store. He knew he had only ten minutes to get checked out, get in his car and make an appointment a few miles away. He began to feel the familiar tightening in his chest and in his fists. He noticed at the checkout counter an older woman chatting with the cashier and he began to get really annoyed and angry. Then he noticed that the older woman was holding a young baby and he saw the older woman hand the baby to the cashier. The line was not moving. Joe was getting more and more angry. To his credit, he tried remembering some of the tools he'd been learning in his mindfulness class and he began to breathe, slowly. He tried to watch his angry feelings and he began to calm himself just a bit. He was able, even a little, to begin to watch the parade rather than to march in it.

By this time the line was moving and, when he reached the cashier, he surprised himself and said "Cute baby!" The cashier smiled gratefully. "Isn't she beautiful?" She went on: "My husband died six months ago in Iraq and I had to go back to work and my mother brings the baby in every day so I can get to see her..."

Some years ago I was greeting people on a Friday night at an Opening the Heart workshop and "Paul" walked in. Because I had read the autobiographical data he sent us some weeks before, I knew that he'd served three tours of duty in Afghanistan and that his wife was divorcing him. His life was falling apart. So I was not surprised or judgmental about his withdrawn, angry body language when he walked into the room. I greeted him warmly and thanked him for writing to us.

His "walls" stayed firmly in place until Saturday afternoon when the dam broke and he sobbed like a child for all he'd seen and lost. I just held him until his breathing slowed. He said he felt "broken". I pointed out that that was a feeling, and that I totally understood, and I also suggested that there is a difference between "feeling" broken and being broken. He'd had no other way to deal with all the pain and grief except to keep it locked up inside. I suggested that the tears were a good way to release the pain. The tears were not that pain itself. That, the pain, had gone in over a long period of time. His body and face softened and he cried again.

These two stories are a lesson to me that when we can pay attention and are able to be back in the present, that we are able to better face the demons, fear and anxiety about the past. It occurs to me that one way of doing this is what I call "using an app". The way this works is that when we experience a judgment (and then, invariably, a trigger), we apply the app by making up a compassionate story about what we "think" we're seeing. It goes like this: 'Judgment, App, Compassion'. So we see not an angry, insensitive person, but someone who is suffering and deserves our understanding and loving attention. We actually make a conscious decision about what it is that we see in front of us. And that changes everything!

Completing the Circle

Reflecting on the circle of my own life cycle.

...And the end of all our exploring will be to arrive where we started and know
the place for the first time.   ~ T.S. Eliot

So I turn around and know that I will soon begin my seventh decade. Yes, they're all true- all the cliches- like "it seems just such a short while ago" I was swimming through my father's legs in the ocean at Nantasket Beach; or "It really has gone by so fast." And now I'm a grandfather of two of the most delightful dancing Beings of Light: Ivy, eighteen months and Marlowe, two and a half years. Don't worry, I'm not going to bore you with stories about how cute or incredibly bright they are. When people my age that I haven't seen for a while, learn I'm a grandfather, almost every time they say "Isn't it just the best!" Well, just between you and me, no, it isn't the best. It's great, yes, but the best? No. What's the best, for me, is watching my son and daughter each parent their little girl.

I think that when any one of us is born, that life begins an arc, a journey, if you will. That beginning marks the start of a circle. Any arc, mathematicians tell us, eventually comes back to itself, completing a circle. And my belief is that there is something hopeful, redemptive even, about a circle being completed. It's both quite simple and beautiful.

I watched my daughter, Abby, one evening giving Marlowe her dinner. Marlowe is smart, beautiful and loving. At this particular dinner time she was also exhausted. Some parents call it "breakdown time". She finished eating what she wanted and then decided she wanted something else that was not on the dinner menu, so she, understandably, began a tantrum. Watching Abby hold her ground in a loving and skillful way was amazing: "Lovey, throwing food is not okay! Just say 'All done' and we can go take a warm bath. Do you want to give Bunny or Baby a bath, too?" Abby never lost her cool, never yelled, kept to her reasonable limits and held the love between them.

On another day, I was reading outside and twenty feet away I was aware of my son, Ari, lying in the grass doing something quietly with Ivy for at least a half hour. I didn't want to interrupt, but I was intrigued, so I quietly went over and saw my son dropping different size pebbles into a bowl of water: "Listen to the sound of the bigger stones as they plop into the water, Ivy." Then he would imitate the sound for her by popping his finger from his mouth. Ivy smiled, reached into the bowl and picked out a stone and dropped it in the bowl again and again. He was teaching her a quiet, mindful meditation about sound and love.

Please don't get me wrong. I am not meaning to pat ourselves on the back for having taught Good Parenting. Neither of these examples is something I ever did when our kids were little. I'm also very aware that, as a parent, the arc of our children's lives always depends, to some extent, on luck and the grace of God. The great choices our kids made for life partners matters a lot, too. Jess, my son in law, Lily my daughter in law, are beautiful people and loving, skillful parents.

I guess I'm just, in a self reflective moment, in the arc of my own life, expressing tremendous gratitude for all the blessings I have been given, and, as I think about the next cycle of life circles, I feel happy about the kind of parents that Ivy and Marlowe may one day be.

Your Tern, My Turn: A Morning Beachwalk

Even in the middle of perfect beauty, the struggle between busy and quiet mind goes on.

Okay, so as well as I can measure it out, these are the ingredients, for me, of a perfect morning. Place: the beach from Baker's Beach to the Westport River, Westport, Massachusetts. Time: early morning, sun has just climbed above the scrub pine, east on Gooseberry Island. Weather: (very important)- 64 degrees, moderate offshore wind, visibility, forever. You can see Cuttyhunk Island way off on the furthest southeastern horizon. Scenery effects: low tide, no one else in site, no music, no phone, osprey fishing for breakfast; one baby osprey, high-pitched caw, maybe out for its first solo flight- what a morning to learn to take wing; a group of mallards, with families, just going for a sea ride; gulls, soaring, dropping sea clams on the rocks; sandpipers chasing the waves in and out. Perfect!

Then, attention, the mind, shifts to Imperfection. What does the psychologist Jon Kabbat Zinn say "Wherever you go, there you are!" So, NBM starts (Negative, Busy Mind): worry, fear, anxiety. Really!? In this perfect place and perfect time? Come on! Okay, do what you've been trained to do: breathe, bring your attention to NBM with some curiosity: "Isn't that interesting- even in this perfect moment, there are negativities, judgments and shit!"

Attention refocuses on the incredible sparkle of the sun's reflection off the water. The osprey and gulls, the wind all, still, seem to be in perfect harmony, untouched by my NBM. And for a few minutes it *works*! I am back in the serenity and beauty of the moment. For a few minutes- really!?.... Yup! Breathe, pay attention to whatever is before me. AND, remember, Jon, everything you've been taught: the goal of mindfulness is not to make one thing stay- not to hold on to one inner state. Breathe and 'Isn't it interesting: even with practice, we cannot aim to hold on to One Dear Thing'.

Then, as I approach the river, something quite wonderful happens. As I walk along the riverbank, with the water emptying into the sea, the wind picks up and there is a huge flock of terns flying upriver, in the same direction I'm walking, just about at the same speed. They fly and dart, and, then, quite suddenly, one drops straight down into the river and then flies up with a minnow in his beak. He carries it to his wife on the shore and tells her to bring it to the "kids".

The whole scene took my breath away. Yes, the intrusive thoughts still occasionally came back. My turn was to stay with those thoughts and then it was Your Tern, and the elegance and poise of the terns took hold. It became a game, not a struggle to make something else happen than what was before me in every moment. And I had an awareness that this walk was, really, no different than any other piece of my life unfolding, and I simply turned to the terns, bowed and gave thanks to God for this moment.

Gratitudes

My first book, *Sitting in the Circle* (2013) was a once in a lifetime opportunity to do a collaboration with my son, Ari, a very talented and accomplished graphic designer. He very much wanted to do an encore with this book but life had other good plans for him: two young children, a loving marriage, a new job and a new house. Nevertheless, I am grateful for his loving support, encouragement and advice. His work can be found at ariberenson.com

Cindy Gorriaran is a dear friend and a gifted graphic designer. She has an active spiritual practice and she knew exactly what I wanted to accomplish in the publication of this book. I thank her for her many hours of creativity, guidance and professional judgment.

I thank my wife, Ruthi, who is the most creative person I know. She has re-created herself many times in this incarnation and what she is most gifted at is the blessing of creating love- in her work, her art and in her community of Loved Ones.

JB

Bibliography

Dalai Lama Tenzin Gyatso. *An Open Heart*. Little Brown and Co., 2002

Estes, Clarissa Pinkola, Ph.D. *Women Who Run With the Wolves*. Bantam Books, 1992

Ferrucci, Pierro. *The Power of Kindness*. Penguin Group, 2007

Housden, Roger.   *Ten Poems to Change Your Life*. Harmony Books, 2001
                    Ten Poems to Open Your Heart. Harmony Books, 2002
                    Ten Poems to Change Your Life Again and Again. Harmony Books, 2007

Kornfield, Jack. *A Lamp in the Darkness*. Sounds True, 2011

Ladinsky, Daniel. *I Heard God Laughing: Renderings of Hafiz*. Sufism Reoriented,1996

Neihardt, John G. *Black Elk Speaks*. Brown Books, 1932

Nye, Naomi Shihab, *You and Yours*. BOA Editions, Ltd., 2005

Seligman, Martin. *Authentic Happiness*. Atria Paperback, 2002

Thich Nhat Hanh. *Peace Is Every Step*. Bantam Books, 1991

Printed in the United States
By Bookmasters